The word "cybernet... Greek word, *kybernetes*, meaning a helmsman, a man who steers his ship to port. The word Dr. Maltz coined, *psycho-cybernetics*, means to steer one's mind to a productive, useful goal.

Psycho-Cybernetics can make the vital difference!

All of us face frustrations in our daily lives, but it is how we deal with them that makes the vital difference between success and failure. Some persons limit themselves, forever keeping themselves from achieving their highest potential. These are persons with low opinions of themselves, with limited expectations. All of us respect and admire someone of quite a different nature—the man who derives great satisfaction as he achieves the goals he sets for himself.

How does he do it?

Dr. Maxwell Maltz reveals to you, one step at a time, *The Creative Secret of Success* in practical, realistic terms that can change your life immediately!

"An important and valuable contribution to man's knowledge of himself and his ability to improve himself."

—*Lewis Gruber*,
Chairman of the Board, P. Lorillard & Co.

"One of the most remarkable and crucial achievements of modern medical and psychological science."

—*Salvador Dali*

PSYCHO-CYBERNETICS

&

SELF-FULFILLMENT

BY
MAXWELL
MALTZ, M.D.

BANTAM BOOKS
TORONTO • NEW YORK • LONDON • SYDNEY • AUCKLAND

TO ANNE

*This low-priced Bantam Book
has been completely reset in a type face
designed for easy reading, and was printed
from new plates. It contains the complete
text of the original hard-cover edition.*
NOT ONE WORD HAS BEEN OMITTED.

PSYCHO-CYBERNETICS & SELF-FULFILLMENT

*A Bantam Book / published by arrangement with
Grosset & Dunlap, Inc.*

PRINTING HISTORY

*Grosset & Dunlap edition published May 1970
2nd printing . September 1970
3rd printing . November 1970
Bantam edition / April 1973
14 printings through April 1985*

ISBN 0-553-24038-2

Published simultaneously in the United States and Canada

---

*Bantam Books are published by Bantam Books, Inc. Its trade-
mark, consisting of the words "Bantam Books" and the por-
trayal of a rooster, is Registered in U.S. Patent and Trademark
Office and in other countries. Marca Registrada. Bantam
Books, Inc., 666 Fifth Avenue, New York, New York 10103.*

PRINTED IN THE UNITED STATES OF AMERICA

H   22 21 20 19 18

CONTENTS

PART ONE

PART TWO

PSYCHO-CYBERNETICS
&
SELF-FULFILLMENT

PART ONE

1

REACHING GOALS

As we go forward into the second half of the twentieth century, we find ourselves in the midst of a great electronics revolution—computers undertake incredible tasks in industry and in our exploration of outer space we have perfected complicated devices which enable us to haul our astronauts back to safety on earth even under emergency conditions.

At the same time, a revolution takes place in the vast inner space of our minds. For we find evidence that in making man, our Creator has endowed him with a servo-mechanism more wonderful than any electronic brain or guidance system that man has invented—and operating on the same basic principles.

Our Creator has given us all a built-in goal-striving device with which to achieve our goals. In the final analysis, this should enable us to rise above the mere physical survival aspect of living to a form of successful, satisfying living.

For animals life implies physical survival as well as the procreation of the species. Thus we find that birds in wintertime fly to warmer climates in self-protection—and their flights of thousands

3

of miles they undertake without even getting hold of the TV weather reports. And a squirrel born in the spring will, without ever having experienced a winter, collect nuts for the winter for survival.

Animals, however, do not select their goals. Their goals of procreation and self-preservation are pre-set.

Human beings, on the other hand, have advanced beyond the animal stage. We possess a power of creative imagination which makes us more than creatures—creators. And, because of this productive imaginative power our goals are limitless.

Within your midbrain is a very small electronic computer, a tape recorder, an automatic servo-mechanism, a success mechanism that you operate like an electronic computer, a goal-striving mechanism that will help you move toward your goals. Like an astronaut whizzing toward his goal somewhere so far away—and returning to earth —you may grope within the vast inner space of your mind to discover the wealth within you before you return to yourself. Not only can your brain function automatically to help you solve problems, but it also can help you adapt more acceptably to life, giving you insight into human behavior, with one overriding goal in view—your complete fulfillment as a human being.

I call this creative psycho-cybernetics, or steering your mind to a productive goal. This does not imply that man is a machine, but that man controls a machine that is his. In my book *Psycho-Cybernetics* I explain this in great detail.

Within us, however, we have, in addition to a success mechanism, a failure mechanism. This failure mechanism is a composite of frustrated, negative feelings which pull us off course, side-tracking our positive inclinations, shrinking our self-image, blocking our attempt to reach our full stature as dignified human beings.

For example, I sit at a table and pick up a spoon. I pick it up in my hand effortlessly. But was this always so? No. As a child, I doubtless dropped my spoon many times until I learned how to pick it up. Then I forgot the many failures to pick up the spoon but remembered the successful perform-ance, stored this in the tape recorder of my mind . . . and now I pick up my spoon successfully.

Thus to reach a goal in the present, you call upon your past experiences the total of which are stored in the electronic computer in your mid-brain. If you reach back to past successes, you reawaken confidence to succeed in the present. But if you go back to past failures, you defeat yourself.

If you move toward failure, you distort your self-image. You dislike and distrust yourself. You fail to guide yourself properly.

The solution? Upgrade yourself; stop down-grading yourself. See yourself in your best mo-ments; do not let success die. Keep on visualizing these good moments—no matter how few—and doggedly focus on these wonderful success pic-tures until you incorporate them into your basic personality.

You live in two worlds. In one world you see darkness and gloom, foreboding and failure, and catastrophe is always around the corner. In the second world your eyes see sunshine, the fields are green, the sky is blue, and your prospects seem brighter each moment.

Let us project ourselves into this second world —of happiness. Let us do this by gearing ourselves to reach out toward our goals.

This is the first chapter in this discussion of ours on how to go about achieving self-fulfillment.

And one fundamental way we do this is to harness our energies and direct them at our goals.

FORWARD TO OUR GOALS

And so, forward to our goals, and let us make an adventure of this exercise, because adventure is fun and fun is a goal in itself.

Here, spelled out again, because I believe that such a procedure crystallizes things more readily in our minds, is our formula for moving toward goals:

1.	R	Reach for Today's Opportunities.
2.	E	Exercise Your Rights to Succeed.
3.	A	Awareness of Your Real Potential.
4.	C	Courage.
5.	H	How to Jump Hurdles.
6.	I	Improvement.
7.	N	Nourishment for Your Self-Image.
8.	G	Going Forward.
9.	G	Getting Places.
10.	O	Observance Day.
11.	A	Anticipation.
12.	L	Learning How.
13.	S	Seeing Yourself Successful.

Ready? Set? Let's go.

1. Reach for today's opportunities

You forget yesterday's blunders; you stop worrying about the past. Today is the day, and you reach out toward today's opportunities.

We are all fragile, sensitive human beings. We are more easily hurt by our failures and by the way others react to us than we like to admit. Still, the business of life is in the present. Opportunities exist for us in the present, and we must reach out to grasp them as eagerly as a baby clutches for its mother or a football tackle takes out after the ball carrier.

Every day is a challenge to you, and you respond to this challenge with the best that is in you. You reach out toward the world, setting your goals, delineating their limits, choosing your methods of moving toward them, then taking action. These goals of the day, these opportunities of the day—make a habit of reaching out toward them.

Do not surrender this excitement, this excitement of reaching out toward opportunities—to overcome negative feelings. Negative feelings, no goal—same thing. You render yourself stationary. You have not broken a leg, yet you place your leg in a cast and you cannot move.

Give yourself a sense of direction and crystallize your opportunities. Move toward your destination, instead of languishing on a merry-go-round.

A goal implies desire and when you feel this desire acutely enough you give yourself an atomic power that will help propel yourself toward the opportunities that the day brings. You insist on fulfilling yourself; you will not take no for an answer.

2. Exercise your right to succeed

Perhaps you cried when you were ushered into this huge world of ours, but crying will do you no good now. You must do more than set goals; you must cultivate in yourself the determination to reach them, and the feeling that you have a right to succeed.

How do you exercise this right?

First, you realize that *you* must instill this

feeling in yourself—the feeling that you are worthy of success, that you deserve the good things.

Second, you build belief in yourself and as you do this, you reactivate the success mechanism —the servo-mechanism—within you. This implies that your eyes are open to opportunities that arise because you want to see them and reach them— without stepping on other people's toes, but also without tripping over your own toes.

Opportunity knocks, but are you listening? Or are you deaf to opportunity, deaf because you cannot exercise your right to succeed, because fear holds you in paralysis?

You must learn to free your senses.

You must learn to see and hear and smell opportunity.

You must exercise your right to succeed. This involves no running around the block, no bicycling or tennis playing, no pushups—it is not that kind of exercise.

But just as physical exercise can be most stimulating for you if you like it and are in con- dition for it, so can this exercise—of your right to succeed.

Too many people fail because they feel they should fail. Too many people fail because they do not believe they have the right to succeed. Too many people defeat themselves.

Don't do this! Reach out toward your goals directly. If you feel you are reaching out for an apple on someone else's apple tree, you will feel like a robber. But this is *your* apple tree! Give your- self your just rights!

3. Awareness of your real potential

You must make yourself aware of your inner strengths and of your basic identity—of what you have done in the past and what you might do in the present and the future.

This is strengthening, this awareness, this re-awakening, this reintegrating of the forces within you.

Let me tell you a story:

In a way it's about my father, and my relationship to my father, whom I loved very dearly. I will tell you about him later on—about his Old World ways in dressing fashionably, and the inspiration which it gave him to help people in our neighborhood on New York City's Lower East Side, and about his tragic death—but that will come later.

Anyway, I was at Naples airport waiting for the London plane one day many years ago. Looking around me at the other passengers, I saw a small stocky man. He was dressed rather formally, in old-fashioned clothes, and he was very neat-looking. He had dark eyes, black hair, and a broad face with beaked nose.

He fascinated me. Where had I seen him before? I wondered. Or had I seen him before?

On the plane we found ourselves seated across the aisle from each other so I had further occasion to observe him. There was no question about it; he reminded me of someone. But who?

I lectured in London, then went on to New York. Back to my practice, and to a heavy, demanding workload that had accumulated in my absence.

One day, tired after a number of tough days, I sat down and glanced at a picture of my father on my side table. I began thinking of him, of his life, and of the sudden tragedy that had taken his life. As I brought the past back into my mind, I felt very close to him again.

Enough of thinking. I went to keep my final appointment for the day.

When I saw the man waiting for me I was astonished. It was the short, stocky, old-fashioned man I'd noticed so curiously on the plane.

He pointed to his ears and nose; they might be improved, he said, and this could help him in his business. He had asked people on the plane who I was, he said. Somehow he had felt a bond of sympathy between us and he had decided he wanted me to perform the operation.

I operated on him soon after—in the morning —and that evening dropped by to visit him, while his face was enmeshed in bandages. It became a habit; each day I dropped by to talk to him since our talks were so pleasant.

Then we took off the bandages and surprise swept over me once again. Staring at his new nose, new ears, and the mustache he had grown while convalescing, I knew why he had so intrigued me. I thought, come back to life almost —my father! The resemblance was almost unbelievable.

"Aren't you from Austria?" I asked him.

"Yes."

"Would you tell me your business?"

"I am a fabric-designer."

"I knew a fabric-designer once," I said, and I could see my father in his neat, formal, old-fashioned clothes. "He came from Austria too."

And, in a flash, the past and present seemed to come together. I felt myself once again a young man in his early twenties, but with one enormous difference: now I felt, more than ever before, how much I had loved my father, how much I had missed him, and how much I would always be in his debt—as long as I lived.

And in this new awareness, this new awakening, this new reintegration of myself, I felt a new potential in myself and I felt that I could reach out toward new frontiers in my life; I felt that I could cross old borders and venture forward into life with a new strength.

Toward new goals. Reaching out toward these goals with stronger arms.

And so can you—when you put together the most positive forces in your life, the most positive forces in you, realizing your true potential, developing it so that you can move forward toward *your* goals.

4. Courage

You must have courage or you will never set out after goals. For suppose you fail, what then? And the answer comes back: If you fail, you must fortify yourself with the courage to take it on the chin and bounce back again into the ring, ready to slug it out.

In a very real sense, life is a series of calculated risks; to survive with satisfaction, you must have courage. You must be courageous enough to surmount your feelings of uncertainty, and to plunge forward after your goals.

Courage means talking over your hopes and your problems with friends who will be willing to share their courage with you. It means coming out of yourself to give your courage to others. It means a concentrated capacity to start all over again when everything goes wrong. It means realizing that you must do more than recognize your strengths; you must also come to peace with your weaknesses. It means moving toward your goals in spite of the obstacles that may rear up in front of you.

Sure you are weak and fragile sometimes— you are only a human being—but at other times you are the Rock of Gibraltar. You are determined; you will not give up easily.

Courage means that a feeling of expectancy urges you on. You are an explorer seeking an uncharted side of yourself. Your hope is not passive; your kinetic force urges you on.

5. How to jump hurdles

Setting goals is not enough; moving toward them is not enough. Your progress toward your goals will seldom be smooth. Golf is not the only game with sand traps to overcome. To achieve your goals, you will have to fight your way out of your sand traps—and then jump your hurdles, too.

Let me tell you another story—about a hurdle jumper. He was a hurdle jumper in college—a magnificent athlete—and he won many medals. His friends admired his athletic ability and one offered him a job as a salesman for his insurance company.

He accepted the job and held it, but never did really well as an insurance salesman. Likeable, with many friends, married, with a son, he could not seem to unleash the drive in him as a hurdle jumper into selling insurance. He feared his imperfections as a salesman and potential customers discouraged him too easily. In college he overcame his own imperfections to become a great hurdler through tenacity and will power; he forgot to use the same approach to overcoming hurdles in selling insurance.

He met his college classmates again at a reunion, and they urged him to try jumping hurdles to see if he could still do it. With a drink or so in him, he borrowed some sneakers and gave it a try. Result: He broke his leg.

The leg was in a cast for a month, and during this period he took stock of himself. Why had he tried jumping the hurdle again when he was too old and out of practice he asked himself. And he recalled how he had overcome his mistakes when he was an expert hurdler: with sense of direction, practice, and more practice. Why then could he not jump the hurdle of living, jump the hurdle of selling insurance? Why couldn't he be a winner at that, too?

When the cast was removed from his leg, he applied himself to selling insurance with the same approach he had used as an athlete: practice and more practice. In his mind he figured out the hurdles he would have to jump: how to tackle the customer, how to deal with his objections. And, with this new approach, he shortly became a winner as an insurance salesman.

You, too, you must do more than set your goals. You must anticipate the hurdles and learn how to overcome them.

6. Improvement

Reaching out toward goals implies a great desire for improvement. You want to better yourself; you want to strengthen your self-image. You want new horizons for yourself; you want to give your life full meaning.

You keep trying to use your imagination creatively in pursuit of the improvement you seek as you reach out toward your goals. Perhaps you feel anxiety, but you do not let anxiety defeat you. On the contrary, you use your anxiety productively; it keeps you moving toward your objectives.

Improvement means clear, rational thinking channelized into creative performance directed at goal achievement.

You wake up in the morning and you set a goal for that day: improvement. A good start.

7. Nourishment for your self-image

In your daily resolve to improve yourself, you find vitamins to fortify your self-image. This will be a good day; your self-image will flourish today.

In setting goals for yourself, you feed your self-image. You give it a framework in which to function; you give it body and substance.

You yearn to get to the better side of yourself —to the confident, compassionate, responsible person you sometimes are. You eagerly seek out opportunities for self-fulfillment, not dead ends which will leave you frustrated. When external pressures mount, you bring up internal strength to meet them: seeing in your mind your past successes.

You devote your day to giving nourishment to your self-image.

Then, when you hit the pillow at night, you recall how during the day you gave your self-image a boost. Recall this—placidly, pleasantly— and chances are you will have little trouble getting a good night's sleep.

8. Going forward

Whether you like it or not, life is movement —and you must keep pace. You cannot live in your yesterdays, when you felt sheltered and safe, without distorting your reality perception. Perhaps your childhood is comforting to think about; perhaps then you felt there was little to fear, but you can't really recapture it. Not to live in again, anyway.

So you must go forward. Out into the world. As you go, you grow. Because you refuse to go into hiding; you tell yourself you're not a criminal.

As you keep going forward, you may find yourself groping and gambling. That's the way things often are. Hopefully, your gambling is wise and creative. You are not playing cards or the stock market. You are gambling on yourself. You are gambling with the blue chips inside you: your confidence, your desire, your self-respect.

Each day you keep moving toward your goals. Each day you move forward, trying to minimize life's gambles as you call on your inner resources to move you toward your goals. On the stock market, stocks may go up and down, but your blue chips can help you soar to new heights.

You have wings—yes, wings. The wings of confidence that can propel you to your goal. Next stop: happiness. And why should you stop yourself if you want to fly?

9. Getting places

Setting goals, moving to achieve them, we find we are getting places. We refuse to sabotage ourselves with ego-destructive criticisms of our failures. What good is such destructive self-mutilation? Instead we keep getting places, and we keep reminding ourselves where we have been.

Stop twirling around in meaningless circles —and insist on getting places—toward worthwhile goals.

So much in life is a product of determination. In the field of the novel, for example, we have Theodore Dreiser, author of *The American Tragedy*, the Cowperwood series, *Sister Carrie*, and so on.

Now Dreiser was an amazing phenomenon —a great novelist, one of the giants in the history of the American novel, and yet even in the opinion of his most ardent admirers he was an awkward, rambling writer who has given us few stylistic delights. Indeed, literary critics eyed him with something like horror; his writing was sometimes of such poor quality that they found it painful to rank him with the giants.

Yet they did.

Why?

Because Theodore Dreiser was a writer of passion. He launched himself upon his writing. He insisted upon getting places with it. He loved to write. He could not live without writing. He started writing and he could not stop. He wrote with heart; he put everything he had and everything he knew into his novels. And one might say that Dreiser, in his passion, in his enthusiasm for his goal—the creation of a novel—smashed forward to his goal. He would not take no for an answer. He would not let critics discourage him. And he even won some of the critics over to his side.

For reluctantly, though continuing to criticize his awkward rambling phrasing, they nevertheless ranked him with the best, because they could not miss the breadth of his sincerity, they could not miss his passion for the feel of life breathed onto his pages, and they could not help but admire his enthusiasm for his characters and for their interactions and for the world which so fascinated him —with which he fascinated the world.

And so—clumsily, unevenly—Theodore Dreiser got places—because this is what he insisted upon. Imperfect, he moved toward his goals, and succeeded.

10. Observance Day

Each year we have many days which we celebrate—we have Mother's Day and Father's Day, and so on.

I now propose a new day. Observance Day.

Observance Day? Observance of what?

Observance of your self-image.

And, on second thought, let me rename my day. Suppose we call it Self-Image Day.

This is your day; this is your big day. For on this day you pull your name off the Loser's List and you tack it up on the Winner's List. A great day! Champagne flows, and there is dancing in the streets.

Don't bother to buy yourself a present! The only present you give yourself is a roundtable discussion with your self-image. And then, you can observe the anniversary of the first Self-Image Day. But that will come later.

On this day you are a friend to yourself. If you live in a cold-water flat six stories up in a walkup, you still feel like a king and as you stagger breathlessly up the stairs you are on your way to your castle. For it is Self-Image Day, and you are King.

It is a great day, Self-Image Day—no confetti, no parades, no announcements on television, but *you feel great.*

And what do you feel so great about? About yourself.

That's quite a goal to achieve any day.

11. Anticipation

Creative anticipation incorporates effort and effort means trying. And, remember this: When you try, you are almost there. You anticipate your arrival because you are in motion, and you come closer and closer to your destination as you move.

With anticipation, you move toward your objective and you move along the main highway. No abandoned road for you, and no dead end! You anticipate the achievement of your goals.

You are cautious as you move because you

refuse to be foolhardy and make needless mistakes. Therefore you stop at red lights, and wait.

But, when you get the green light, you accelerate. You drive forward, you surge forward, you launch yourself forward. Even now, though you drive safely. No foolish accidents for you! You insure your safety with clear thinking, with constant reappraisals of your strategies, with continual reinforcement of your self-image.

As long as you have the gift of life, you anticipate. As long as you are able to breathe, you anticipate. And why shouldn't you? God made you to live, and to have rights.

12. Learning how

You must learn how to move toward your goals, how to live with your goals, how to accept failure, and how to live with success and achievement.

Goal orientation takes know-how, and it takes a lot of learning how. You must learn what to do to get to your goals; you must also learn what not to do.

Watch a top ballerina. Precision. No waste motion. Brilliant performance. And that is her goal.

You learn how to move toward your goals when you negotiate with your fears and bring about the retreat of negative feelings.

Constantly, you seek to learn how to make the most of your assets, how to strengthen your self-image, how to march through the desert of negative feelings to fruition.

Naturally, as you take out after your goals, you try not to get in a too-vulnerable position, but still you must often take your chances in this world and you know this.

13. Seeing yourself successful

If you set realistic and worthwhile goals and then move toward them fearfully, chances are that you will go nowhere. To reach your goals, you must see yourself successful.

You will help yourself march on your goals when you bring out of your storehouse of memories your images of your past successes, so that you see yourself as a successful individual, so that you feel yourself as a successful individual, so that your imagination is alive with success pictures.

Bring these success images back into your imagination, reconstruct them with tender and loving care, and you may move on your goals with confidence.

ACHIEVING YOUR DAILY VICTORIES

And so, in this first chapter, we have discussed how to reach goals.

O. Henry once wrote a charming short story called *The Third Ingredient*. The main plot is simple and unpretentious. A stalwart, indomitable woman in her early thirties finds herself without a job and almost penniless. She has just bought some beef from the butcher and goes to the brownstone in which she lives to cook it. Her spirit is not crushed by her misfortunes but, she laments, what good is beef without potatoes and an onion? And, aggressively, almost militantly, she goes after the missing ingredients. They become her daily goal—and she moves after them in a dogged way which could serve as inspiration and guide to anyone reading this delightful story.

Anyway, *she* finds her missing ingredients, and I hope that, in reading this chapter and this book, *you* will absorb the ingredients that go into making goals attainable.

You will, I feel confident, be a happier person if you can kindle enough desire to want to achieve goals—and to want to implement this desire every day with positive action.

I wish you daily victories—in achieving your goals and in moving toward greater self-fulfillment as you achieve them.

2

THE FULFILLMENT IN YOUR
SELF-IMAGE

Each day you wake up in the morning and there you are—once again in your own little world. You prepare for your day in the many superficial ways that are habits for you—washing, showering, shaving, powdering, breakfasting—but what will this day bring you?

Frustration—or self-fulfillment?

Perhaps I should rephrase this: What will *you* bring to *yourself* this day—frustration, or self-fulfillment? Because you are not helpless and passive, chances are; your day does not just happen to you. You must make yourself responsible for the caliber of your day.

And, by implication, you must make yourself responsible for the caliber of your many days, your many weeks, your many months, your many years.

In these pages we will assume that you wish to exercise this responsibility wisely, in the service of your best friend—yourself—and that you wish to plot a sure path leading to many days of self-fulfillment. Indeed, to a lifetime of fulfillment.

That is our goal, and we will mass our

energies in the accomplishment of this worthy goal, using the principles of psycho-cybernetics.

That is our goal—self-fulfillment—and let us now muster up our energies to achieve this goal.

We will now discuss your greatest asset or greatest liability—your self-image. For a strong self-image is almost synonymous with self-fulfillment, and a weak self-image is almost synonymous with frustration.

What is your self-image? Well, you can't see it, you can't touch it, you can't taste it—but nonetheless it is real. It is as real as the chair you sit on as you read this. It is as real as the hands with which you turn the pages. It is as real as real can be.

Your self-image is *your* picture of yourself. It is *your* opinion of yourself. It is *your* value judgment about yourself. And this image of yourself you carry with you out into the world; it helps shape the caliber of your experiences.

On this day of yours you step out into the world. It is, by and large, not an easy world. It is an uncertain place—full of wrangling, manipulating, hopeful, hopeless people, excitable people, I would say, people seeking something.

Seeking what?

Self-fulfillment.

Will they find it? It depends largely on their approach. If an individual expects miracles to be showered on him, he will probably be disappointed. I doubt if anyone will walk up to him in the street and hand him a hundred-dollar bill just to make his day pleasant. And probably he will not become world-famous overnight—except perhaps in his dreams.

What you need as you step out into this uncertain world is not an external miracle, a stroke of good fortune—though these may help once in a while—but an internal strength firing you from within.

This strength you will feel only when you build your self-image. You will feel it only when you learn to like your picture of yourself as you move around your little world. It will be real strength only when you are kind toward yourself, when you are a friend to yourself, when you refuse to quit on yourself. Its reality will depend on the picture of yourself that you see alive in your imagination.

THE DUAL FORCES IN YOU

Now let us turn to a little exercise in spelling; we will spell out for you the dual forces in you that can strengthen or weaken your self-image. These forces are crucial; to be happy, you must bolster the positive forces and fight off the desire for defeat and negation.

1. **Y** You or Somebody Else.
2. **O** Obey or Oppose.
3. **U** Unbelief or Understanding.
4. **R** Resentment or Reason.

5. **S** Stranger or Friend.
6. **E** Enthusiasm or Extinction.
7. **L** Live or Perish.
8. **F** Fact or Fiction.

9. **I** Indecision or Decision.
10. **M** Mind Watcher or Mind Avoider.
11. **A** Adjustment or Atrophy.
12. **G** Go-Go or No-No.
13. **E** Enterprise or Emptiness.

Here is YOUR SELF IMAGE, spelled out, and now we will tackle our subject under these thirteen headings. And don't let the supposedly terrifying number thirteen frighten you. Today we will make it your lucky number.

1. You or somebody else

Who are you? You look at yourself in the mirror. Fine, but who is this face? Who are you? Are you a self-directed person, strong enough to live your life, or are you a person who feels his worthlessness and spends his time dodging and turning, trying to please Joe and Mary and Harry, remodeling his personality repeatedly in his attempts to please, reshaping his image of himself so often that he has lost track of who he really is.

You must come to grips with yourself. You must each day—if only for a little while—shake off your responsibilities and fight off your pressures and let yourself think about the most important person in the world—you. How are you doing? Your physical self is surviving, but how about your identity? Are you you or are you somebody else? Are you strong enough to be you?

You must understand that happiness comes from accepting yourself for the imperfect person you are. When you spend your days trying to imitate somebody else, you tarnish the good image of yourself that you can build and cherish.

Stop measuring yourself by the standards of other people! Use your own standards.

Stop trying to imitate your favorite movie star or athlete or politician! Make your own movies —in the form of success pictures on the moving-picture screen of your imagination. Who is the hero? You. Who is the adventurer who seeks to make each day a better one? You. Who operates the motion picture projector, fearlessly showing truth for you to see? You.

Not somebody else. You.

2. Obey or oppose

Do you obey? Or do you oppose? PLAY BALL! That is the name of the game. In any athletic contest you follow rules. Baseball, football, golf, soccer, basketball, hockey—they all have rules. You play tennis and as the ball goes back and forth, back and forth, you keep your eye on the ball. You obey the rules of the game; you do not oppose them.

It is just as vital to play ball with your self-image. Give yourself a break, especially when you're behind. When you make a mistake, stop telling yourself how miserable you are as a person. Aren't you more than a blunder? Be human with yourself; and play ball with yourself.

Obey the rules of your fine game: building your self-image. Give up your obstructionist opposition.

Give in to the rational knowledge that you are a human being of worth, that you have rights, and that you owe it to yourself to forgive your human imperfections.

Give in to—and obey—the rational knowledge that you have just as much right to see good in yourself as the other fellow.

Do you oppose yourself in your search for a good feeling about yourself? Do you oppose your positive qualities by harping on your weaknesses? Are you holding yourself back from yourself?

Obey the good rules—the rules of the battle for self-fulfillment—and when the umpire dusts off home plate and cries PLAY BALL, get that bat in your hands and belt a home run.

3. Unbelief or understanding

We are all complex people; we are composites. We love and we hate, we laugh and we cry, we believe and we feel disbelief, we understand and we misunderstand.

You may give yourself the benefit of an understanding, compassionate attitude or you may reject the essence of your personality with lack of faith, with disbelief in yourself and your potentials.

Once again, here is a battle between the dual forces inside yourself—your failure drives and your success drives. To strengthen your self-image, you must bring into play understanding—and compassion—to help you support yourself under all circumstances.

You set your goals and move toward them, but you are not perfect and sometimes your mistakes will block you from your goals. This stirs up disbelief in yourself and a hornet's nest of criticism buzzes in your mind.

But why? Why should you inflict upon yourself unbelief? Why should you be so disloyal to yourself just because you made a few mistakes?

Instead, when you are imperfect, give yourself understanding. Understand that we all make mistakes and, under pressure, can lose faith in ourselves. Understand that under difficult conditions we all have an opportunity to show our true worth by giving ourselves compassion, not castigation. Finally, understand that the person with a strong self-image sees failure as part of life; he understands his failures are inevitable, but never regards himself as *a failure*. He rises above his mistakes to new, more seasoned, more mature successes.

You cannot always be just the kind of person you would, ideally, like to be. No one can. Perhaps it will help you if I tell you about a recent day in which I was not my own perfect person, but in which I nevertheless managed to accept myself.

Several patients phoned in for reassurance on the operations I had done for them; I was well aware that they were in good shape and needed only a few comforting words—and I was accustomed to dispensing such comfort—but on this day I felt inadequate to the task. I mumbled a few token words of encouragement and let it go at that.

I ate lunch with friends at a restaurant, dawdled too long, then remembered I was late for an appointment at my office. I rushed for a cab—but the New York crosstown traffic was impossible. I was a half hour late for my appointment. Unforgivable, I mumbled to myself. I tried to console myself with the fact that I am a punctual, responsible person.

This was not my day for efficiency: I had neglected to phone my answering service and, hours late, found a friend had called me and I hadn't called him back. I was short-tempered with my nurse, who short-tempered me back (good for her!). Need I go on? This was not my day.

But, painfully, I accepted myself. With the knowledge that I am imperfect and that some days I will make blunders. And, with the additional knowledge that I have had my successes and that I try to do good and that I have helped others on other, better days.

You, too. On your bad days, give yourself a break. Be a friend to yourself.

4. Resentment or reason

We all live through our daily resentments: perhaps we miss our bus or our train; then, all of a sudden, the rain pours down and, wet and uncomfortable, we marvel at the people all around us who had the foresight to carry an umbrella; a look at our newspaper and we seethe with frustration as we read about endless human strife; finally, a few harsh words from the boss and—

But hold on! We must not let our resentment run wild; we must call on that power for which man is reputedly noted—the power of reason.

"But I am reasonable," you protest. "Bill and Sally and Alice are confused, I guess, but me, I am reasonable."

Sometimes you are. But is it reasonable to allow the flow of minor irritations that are part of almost any day to push you into a mass of resentment? Is it reasonable to keep picturing, over and over in your mind, how you just missed catching your train? Is it reasonable to keep hearing, over and over, a few harsh words of your boss?

Fight off your resentment; use your reason to guide you toward a good day. Forget today's irritations and, especially, stop obsessing yourself with your grievances from yesterday and your many yesterdays.

A year or two ago a woman of forty came to see me in my office. Married, she had two children, but they did not take away her sense of grievance which she carried with her. She came from a family of five, she said, and her mother dominated her, criticizing her repeatedly and apparently liking her other children better. Her mother was an artist, and this woman also liked to paint, but her mother discouraged her, telling her she had no talent. The woman felt worthless.

She deeply resented her mother, she revealed, even though her mother lived one hundred miles away from her. She felt enormous resentment toward her mother.

Was this reasonable? I asked her, to live in the past. What about creative living in the present? She had a family of her own now. How about day-to-day goals with them? How about thinking about that? For the resentment from her past was smothering her present.

"How do I start?" she asked me.

"Four points," I said, "none of them easy—unless you have the desire to make them easy.

"First, forgive others, forgive your mother for *your own* peace of mind.

"Second, forgive yourself—for you have been unkind to yourself, seeing yourself with unkind eyes.

"Third, see yourself at your best. Think of yourself—and picture yourself—as you are when you like yourself. Stop seeing yourself as a failure.

"Fourth, and most important of all, keep up with yourself, not with somebody else. If you like painting, go ahead and paint. Don't try to imitate your mother. Be yourself. Stop making comparisons when you paint. Paint because you want to do it, because you love it, because you need the feeling you get when you paint. If you don't like what you did, start all over again on another canvas. This will be your way to find yourself, to build a belief in yourself. Will you try?"

"I will try," she said.

She was as good as her word.

Eight months later she visited me. She looked wonderful; her face was radiant and she had lost fifteen pounds. She handed me a painting—sad and mournful—of a clown. I studied it and then looked at her.

"That was me," she said. "But look at me now!"

5. Stranger or friend

Every day of your life, with few exceptions, chances are you go out into the world. You walk down the street, and it is not often that you are alone. Many other people also walk down this street; they are strangers to you.

All day long you meet many strangers: on the bus or train, in restaurant or cafeteria, everywhere you go.

These impersonal contacts do not bother you, though, because you have friends in your life. The strangers can remain distant; you do not need them to be close.

How different it is with your self-image! It is a disaster if you are a stranger to yourself; it is a blessing if you are a friend to yourself. Your entire commitment to life depends on your commitment to yourself. You must be closer to yourself than you are to your parents, to your spouse, to your children. You must annihilate the distance that separates you from yourself: this distance can only make you a stranger to yourself, walking in loneliness through the world.

Get to know your self-image. Become conscious that it exists. Become conscious that this image vitally affects your capacity for self-fulfillment—the ways that you act, the ways that other people react to you.

And understand this:

Your actions hinge on your opinion of yourself. If past successes have conditioned you to see yourself in your mind as a successful person, you will feel proud of yourself and will find ways to continue this image. If, on the other hand, you picture yourself as a failure and constantly visualize your past blunders, you are setting yourself up for more failure and more frustration.

Change this image of yourself if it frustrates you; you can change it, and through this productive change, you can begin a new life, a life directed toward success and happiness. It may be hard work—but others have done it. Maybe you can, too.

You must work creatively with a self-image that is not a stranger, but a friend.

Like Harry Truman.

I remember well—do you?—when Franklin Delano Roosevelt passed on and the nation mourned. As with John F. Kennedy later, people reacted in a most personal way,—as if a beloved friend, more than a great President, had left them.

Harry S Truman took office amidst this state of national shock, and his presence in the Presidency seemed to reassure few. Many people I knew did not believe in him as they had in FDR and felt considerable anxiety about his ability to handle the Presidency with full authority. Maybe he looked too much like a man-in-the-street.

But one man believed unswervingly in Harry S Truman.

And he was the only man who had to. Truman himself.

And, in his years in office, President Harry S Truman accepted his overwhelming responsibilities without evasion—even with cheerfulness, it seemed—and some claim that he will go down in history as one of our great Presidents.

My point is this: Harry Truman paid no attention to what others wrote about him or what they said about him. His critics were legion when he took office and had he taken their comments seriously he would have crumbled—well, he didn't. He relied on himself for his strength.

His self-image was his friend.

You, too. Make your self-image your friend.

6. Enthusiasm or extinction

Close your eyes, relax, and get ready for the double feature in the theater of your mind.

First you see a close-up of a person who is frustrated. Tense face, forehead creased in frown, teeth clenched, and hands knotted into fists.

Now a new picture—another close-up, but this person is happy. A smile warms up the face, the eyes glisten, and you can see the palms of both hands.

A double feature, two pictures—and the strange thing is that both of them are you.

For you are a person of enthusiasm, and you are a frustrated person propelling yourself toward extinction.

You are a person who sees the bright side of things one day; and you are a person who sees nothing but disaster and calamity the next day.

You are a person who feels like a winner at one time and in one type of situation, and you are a person who under different conditions loses out.

In choosing your life style, you must move away from the forces of extinction; you must hop on the vehicle that moves you toward an enthusiasm for living.

How do you do this? By working every day to build your self-image.

7. Live or perish

To develop a healthy self-image means to live. Live where? In the present, not in yesterday. In reality, not in fantasy. Living today in yesterday is not living; it is perishing.

Too many people, unfortunately, do not live; they perish. Each day they surrender themselves to futility.

You do this when you:

A. Retreat from life and the world.
B. Give up on your self-image.
C. Surrender to loneliness and despair.
D. Bury yourself in a cycle of resentment.

Years ago I spoke to a woman at a seminar in Arizona; it was a seminar for three hundred dentists and her husband listened as she talked to me.

"I feel miserable," she said.

"Why?"

"I must be abnormal. I can't have children."

"Did you ever think of adopting a child?"

"I don't know—it wouldn't be the same thing."

"Perhaps not, but it might be better."

Three years later this woman wrote me; she had decided to adopt a child and in giving her love to the little child she had found a fulfillment and then found that she could give more love to her husband. No longer did she feel inadequate. No longer did she feel abnormal. No longer did she live the life of half a human being.

She had adopted more than a child; in the process she had adopted herself—as a full human being.

She was perishing; she fought her way back to life.

The death-in-life way is no way to live; you must live or perish. You live when you like yourself. You live when the image you carry in your imagination—the image of yourself—is pleasant and relaxing for you so that you are not afraid to move out into the world in broad daylight.

8. Fact or fiction

We spend so much of our time trying to make certain impressions on others that it is hard to get to know ourselves—as we really are. Not the fictitious self we pretend to be, but the genuine person.

Fact, not fiction, must be our goal. Reality, not masquerade. What is, not what we feel should be.

The trouble is that to live in reality, an individual must like himself—as he really is. If you distrust yourself, if you are ashamed of yourself, if you can't live with yourself, then you will try to be somebody else.

If, on the other hand, you use the confidence of past successes to give you a good feeling about yourself and your present undertakings—then you can accept reality. Then you can devote yourself to living a life of fact, not fiction.

A healthy self-image, this is your key toward achieving life in reality.

9. Indecision or decision

Indecision means doubt and doubt implies fear. Perhaps sometime in the past you made a bad mistake, and you're afraid to repeat this mistake.

But remember this: Because you failed badly once, this does not mean you are a failure as a human being.

Too many of us are undecided. We impale ourselves on the fence of indecision; our goals are

We must overcome this attitude; we must learn to be decisive. We must set goals. We must have the courage to make up our minds. We must have the courage to take a stand. We must make indefinite. We don't know where we're going. decisions.

To do this, we must overcome the fear of past failures. We must also win out over the need to be perfect. Because when we become doers, when we set goals and take action, we make ourselves vulnerable to possibilities of failure. To be decisive, we must be able to accept the bad with the good and keep going.

We move through indecision to decision when we think enough of ourselves to accept ourselves no matter what are the consequences of our actions. Then we can feel the capacity to feel decisive.

10. Mind watcher or mind avoider

We have all kinds of "watchers" these days. We have bird watchers, weight watchers, stock-market watchers, and weather watchers.

Now, how about mind watchers?

The mind watcher is the best watcher of all, to my way of thinking. The mind watcher is keenly aware of the operations in that all-important area —the mind. He is quick to fight off tumors of doubt when they invade. He is quick to ward off the poison of self-contempt when it appears. He is quick to shake off the beginning of obsessive fears of catastrophe when they start to take root.

And, on the other hand, the mind watcher watches for the better side of himself. He stops, looks and listens. He builds in his imagination pictures of his past successes. He constantly works to keep improving his opinion of himself.

The mind avoider loses himself in trivia. He spends his life escaping from himself. He does not think creatively or seek relevance. He ignores his mind; he loses touch with his self-image.

Be a mind watcher! Keep up with yourself! Be a self-image watcher! This is the way to self-fulfillment.

11. Adjustment or atrophy

A proper self-image implies that each day you adjust to the changing conditions in your world—external and internal.

I conducted a seminar in San Diego, California, in creative psycho-cybernetics; more than two hundred students were in the class. One student asked me how long it took for a person to change his self-image, and I told him that it took five minutes or a whole lifetime.

What I meant was that we live with change. Life changes, and your self-image changes. Each day life is different, and you are different, and you must adjust to these changes. Each day, new problems—internal and external—and you must make the necessary adjustments to deal with these changes and move toward your goals.

If you do not adjust, you atrophy. You disable yourself—physically and mentally. You succumb to inertia; you surrender your creative life forces.

Therefore you must adjust to change; you really have no choice.

12. Go-go or no-no

A basic characteristic of a strong self-image is movement—movement into the world of people, creative movement into another stimulating world inside your mind.

Set your goals. Plan your growth. Feel a child's excitement inside your soul. Go-go!

Stop blocking this goal-driving with negative feelings. Stop saying no-no to the things you want to achieve.

If you feel you have rights, if you feel you are worthy of happiness, you will develop these capacities for movement and for growth.

Fortified with a strong self-image, you will say to yourself, go-go! Not no-no!

13. Enterprise or emptiness

And here we are—at lucky number thirteen. Enterprise or emptiness.

You strengthen your self-image through enterprise. Through a daily excitement in your activities. You motivate yourself with your goals, and enterprise indicates your desire to reach your goals.

You must every day treat yourself to a better you. Giving yourself appreciation every day, giving yourself self-acceptance, giving yourself praise, you then are able to launch yourself forward into enterprises with enthusiasm and with a belief in yourself that may make them successful enterprises.

The opposite of enterprise is emptiness—days of boredom, days of apathy, days of non-living even though you have the gift of life.

Each day you must resolve to move toward enterprise, away from the passive emptiness that is one of the tragedies of life today.

THE PRECIOUS IMAGE OF YOU

Your self-image is your pacemaker in your search for self-fulfillment. Without a strong self-image, the search is an illusion.

This image of yourself is precious beyond calculation. No adding machines can total the extreme value of a healthy self-image, and no computers can measure it either.

We are, luckily, most of us, not born in the image of Victor Hugo's grotesque, unfortunate Quasimodo, the hunchback of Notre Dame, the half-blind bellringer of the cathedral, doomed to deafness at fourteen by the demands of his occupation. Quasimodo, with his huge head, mocked by people, howled at by dogs. People would flee at the sight of him; fearing him, they isolated him. It was thought that he could turn men to stone and frighten pregnant women into abortions. His intentions were far better than this —poor Quasimodo—but who knew this?

Chances are overwhelming that physically

you are not a Quasimodo, but how do you see yourself in your mind? Deformed, without rights —like Quasimodo?

Or strong and healthy—as you should see yourself?

Your self-image is your most precious asset. Make it a daily task to build it, to nourish it, to feed it. As a creative mind watcher, work to build this precious asset of yours. Every day of the week. Every day of the year.

And as you work to build this image of yourself, you move toward your self-fulfillment. As a human being in a changing, trying, complicated world, you nevertheless insist on your right to happiness, to achievement, to fulfillment.

3

FULFILLMENT THROUGH
CLEAR THINKING

You work to fulfill yourself. No dilettante are you. You do not expect miracles or help from unknown sources; your help—and you understand this realistically—must come from yourself.

You expect no heavenly intervention in your own behalf; you know very well that no intermediaries on earth will come to bring you everything you need. Other people, too, have their hands full coping with life's problems.

So, to fulfill yourself, in the many todays which constitute your life, you must bank basically on yourself.

You know this, and while this knowledge may take you out of the realm of fantasy and daydreaming into the world of reality, you accept this world for it *is* the world. As a child, you may live with your daydreams and pretend they are real; as an adult, you are through with daydreams.

In this world of reality, in this often difficult world of reality, you bank on yourself—on the strength of your self-image.

And, as we learned, you work to build this key asset of yours—your self-image.

Now we are attempting to build a fine highway, a superb highway, paved with first-class materials, paved with solid materials that will not betray. This highway may or may not lead to New York, to Chicago, to Los Angeles, to St. Louis, to Miami. It *will* lead to your self-fulfillment, chances are; this is the intended destination of our invisible, but oh-so-real highway.

You are working to strengthen your self-image? Good. Your self-image is your base; without it your highway would lead nowhere at all; it would be merely a dead end.

Now let us move forward resolutely—our goal, self-improvement. Self-improvement leading to self-fulfillment. A worthy aim.

Let us turn to a consideration of clear thinking. For, to fulfill yourself, you must learn this art.

The devout and immovably rigid materialist may see little in clear thinking—except as it relates to his quest for tangible possessions. And yet, how can you possibly fulfill yourself without mastering it? How can you feel peaceful inside when your thinking is muddled?

I am not one to undervalue material things; in truth, I like my comforts and possessions.

Still, one must not *overvalue* these material products. And an individual may own house, automobile, the most luxurious furniture, and so on, and feel completely unfulfilled—if his thinking is torturous and confused.

And so we will examine the components of clear thinking, spelling them out for you—so that we can move toward mastery of this most important ability.

THE MEANING OF CLEAR THINKING

First, let us delve further into the meaning of clear thinking.

You must realize, at the outset, that thinking is in itself a worthwhile goal, and that when you cultivate in yourself a desire to reach this goal you are already moving constructively because effort represents the launching pad of accomplishment.

For the desire is your take-off point; this desire is your countdown point, and while your countdown will not result in your rocketing off into outer space, it may enrich your examination of inner space, the inner space in your mind, so important to your happiness.

How do you fire up your desire to think clearly and creatively? You repeat and repeat to yourself your realization that, in pushing to fruition your innate need to live the good life and feel happy, the art of thinking is one of your great gifts. If you neglect it, you neglect yourself. Do you, upon awakening, neglect to eat your breakfast? Then do not neglect to work at building your capacity for clear thinking.

Clear thinking means that you define what you are thinking about and focus your attention upon it.

Clear thinking means that you refuse to get caught up in actions without thinking, but that you think clearly first—and then move into action. However, once you are thinking clearly, you can take action, then improvise as you go.

Clear thinking means that you ask yourself intelligent questions and refuse to crush your innate curiosity. You keep your mind open, refuse to rely passively on the thinking of others. You do not relinquish your creative option; it is too precious.

Clear thinking means that you probe for the hidden assets within you, like a miner seeking precious ore to bring out into the world. It means that you refuse to allow your negative feelings to get out of control and, like a malignant growth, eat up the wealthy area of your mind.

Clear thinking means you are on your way toward constructive achievement.

Through this inestimable gift you find that you can play many roles in your mind and then turn these roles into reality goals. For clear thinking is indeed the launching pad for many goals—for the growth of relaxation, of compassion, of the ability to unlock your genuine personality, and of your capacity to withstand and overcome life's unceasing pressures and problems. Moreover, clear thinking is interlocked and interrelated with your building of a strong self-image.

Your clear thinking is your laboratory. In this laboratory you synthesize raw material into creative thought, then transform this thought into action, in the surehanded knowledge that as you achieve your goals your goals reflect back upon you, enlarging the scope of the confidence inside you, reactivating the functioning of your success mechanism, watering to fruition the proud plants of compassion, humility and self-respect.

Clear thinking implies an understanding not only of your own needs, but of the needs of others. You reach out to comprehend the creative and destructive drives inside yourself and you gear yourself to encourage the constructive drives.

Your clear thinking leads you on to the development of good habits. You work to build up a chain of positive habits that will move toward your reactivating your success mechanism, toward the achievement of mature happiness, toward overcoming life's pressures and turning them into opportunities for expansion and emotional growth.

As you learn to think clearly and creatively, you become your own judge—not a hanging judge, but a sympathetic judge who will be on your side. You atone for your blunders not by succumbing to the horror of guilt, but by forgiving yourself and rising above them.

Understand this, for to achieve self-fulfillment you must understand this: *Creative thinking is the greatest power in the universe.* It is the *summum bonum* of which philosophers have written down through the ages.

You understand, then, the meaning of clear, creative thinking? You understand, then, that if you stop polishing your car (you've polished it only seven times?) and start working on your thinking, polishing *that,* you will not be the loser?

Enough for the meaning. Let us now spell out for each other the components of clear thinking.

THE COMPONENTS OF CLEAR THINKING

Here they are. Read and reread them; I feel confident they will help you.

1. **C** Concentration.
2. **L** Longing for Improvement.
3. **E** Empathy.
4. **A** Aspiration.
5. **R** Relaxation.

6. **T** Tapping Hidden Resources.
7. **H** Habit of Self-Discipline.
8. **I** Imaginative Development of Will Power.
9. **N** Nostalgia—For Today.
10. **K** Knowledge of Direction.
11. **I** Integrity.
12. **N** New Nucleus of Faith.
13. **G** Growth as a Human Being.

Now, suppose we tackle them one by one.

1. Concentration

It is self-evident that one cannot think clearly without concentration. If one's thoughts flicker here and there, never settling to a fixed theme, obviously one's thinking will not achieve real focus.

The iconoclastic, stubborn, creative, brilliant, eccentric Yankee Henry David Thoreau spent over two years living alone at Walden Pond and he credited the isolation with inspiring his concentration upon his studies and upon his thinking.

Fair enough. But you can achieve a fine degree of concentration even in our hustle-bustle world of whizzing cars, blaring radios, and frantic people. With effort, with considerable effort perhaps. But the point is that it can be done.

Concentration is thought massed in formation, like a football line, seven strong, gearing itself in readiness to charge at an opponent, focusing on the weak point through which to charge, so that the ball carrier can push through to his goal.

The concentrated thinker moves forward toward his goal, head-on, searching out his topic thoroughly, seeking out every possibility.

In a recent book I wrote about a young man who lived a solitary life on a faraway island so that he could find himself; so that he, like Thoreau, could use solitude to find life's meaning.

To repeat, this is not necessary. In your reality, in the world you know, in the world that is accessible to you, take the first step toward clear thinking: *Learn to concentrate.*

Take a few minutes off each day and turn off the radio, turn off the television set, shut yourself off from intrusion as best you can, shake your mind free of worry and irritation and trivia, focus on some fruitful area of thinking.

Then concentrate your thinking. When distractions invade your mind, when negative feelings threaten you, fight them off as you would a bee about to sting you.

Your goal is to think—in the purest, most complete way possible—about your subject area. This is an important project for you. Your thinking, your mental processes, these are you.

So, concentrate.

2. Longing for improvement

We all long to better ourselves. Often we point to tangible, visible goals in this quest of ours: bankbooks that chart our financial gains, annual incomes that are demonstrable, shining automobiles that all can see.

But in our longing for improvement we must include an essential: the improvement in the caliber of our thinking.

Let me tell you a story that goes back many years to days when I was an intern in a hospital —and a harassed, overworked, sleepless one at that. Penniless, too, I might add. The intern's life was not one that I could whole-heartedly recommend to those who seek the easy life.

In addition to all my other troubles—such as rude awakenings in the middle of the night when, for some reason, so many pregnant women seemed to give birth—I carried the extra load of a burning resentment. I utterly loathed our most skillful surgeon. I shall call him Dr. B.

I admired Dr. B. How could I help but admire him: with his deft fingers, searching eyes, and quick thinking. He was a magnificent surgeon.

But hate! My hate for this man surged in me like a swollen river about to overflow its banks.

My grievances against him ranged from a disapproval of his noisy clothes (in my then impoverished state, this was mostly envy) to an irritation at his teasing me for my shy, worshipful love of a student nurse and to fury at his insulting my technique one time when I assisted him in an operation. To top it all off, he would come upon me in the hallway, trying to eavesdrop on his telephone conversations, and he would insult me further.

My thoughts toward Dr. B. were full of venom. I thought of revenge—and more revenge. His insults infested my mind; they were, I thought, unforgivable.

Another intern, a friend, joined in my feelings. Dr. B. was, we agreed, a marvelous surgeon, but otherwise a miserable human being.

Then, one day, Dr. B. said he'd like to talk with us. He started off by apologizing for his behavior toward us. Then he began to explain his troubles. It seems a friend had given him a "sure thing" tip on the stock market; he had invested heavily and been rocked for huge losses. One thing had led to another and . . . I listened, unbelievingly, to the woes of the man I had hated, the man I had looked at and weighed and found wanting—and then I realized I had never known him at all.

Dr. B. told us how a father of a child he had operated on had told him how we interns admired his skill as a surgeon. He had been touched by our regard and felt doubly ashamed that he had treated us so shabbily. Contrite, humble, human, he offered each of us a cigar.

What a change there was after this conversation in the hospital! We interns went about our usual activities. The worst crises seemed to summon us, sleepless, from bed between midnight and daybreak, but our thinking, our feeling had improved—and drastically.

Speaking for myself, my resentment was now friendliness and my self-centered irritation was now awareness; there had taken place, overnight, a tremendous improvement in the caliber of my thinking.

Back to my point: that to move toward clear thinking you must long for improvement. You, too, must have the desire to do away with the malignancy of resentment and to improve your thinking.

3. Empathy

We do not think clearly without empathy for others. In the story I just told, about Dr. B., I, as an intern, reacted from an unrealistic, oversensitive point of view. I never cared to think about the underlying reasons that might be responsible for his harsh treatment of me. I lacked empathy.

The empathetic person not only feels for others, he also listens to others. He does not just talk; he also listens to others talk.

The person with empathy rises above self-centered thinking to objective, rational, many-faceted thinking which, unfortunately, is not commonplace. He bursts through the bonds of blind, provincial, prejudiced thinking to clear thinking because he is concerned with all of mankind.

4. Aspiration

Clear thinking means not only that you feel aspiration for your needs, but that you also wish to help others. Your concern for humanity reaches far beyond yourself to encompass your community, your friends, your nation. Your sense of responsibility extends beyond yourself out to all humanity.

Thus William Lloyd Garrison devoted his life to the aspirations of others, rising above questions of self-interest to champion the cause of the millions who in his day were slaves. Garrison ignored the abuse many heaped upon him, the length of the struggle, and his own financial impoverishment to fight for the aspirations of others.

I do not suggest that you go this far in helping others but when you concern yourself with helping others you increase the objectivity—and therefore the clarity—of your thinking.

Aspiration is close to empathy. When you focus on both, you move yourself closer to clear, creative, rational thinking.

5. Relaxation

This is your very own powerhouse. For in relaxation you create a climate in your mind which will allow clear thinking to live and survive. We will deal briefly with relaxation here, and go into greater detail later. But it is obvious that you do not think clearly while a tornado whips back and forth across your mind, whipping you into recurrent frenzies; clear thinking and the self-fulfillment it leads to grow in the soothing climate of a relaxed mind.

6. Tapping hidden resources

To know yourself is not easy. The home-run hitter does not know he is a home-run hitter until he hits some home runs. Until then he may know he is muscular or that he has powerful wrists—but he does not know that he is a home-run hitter.

If you are able to dig into yourself and unearth thoughts and feelings which make you more real and vital to yourself, you bolster your self-image and, in doing this increase your capacity for clear thinking.

Still, you do not live alone; you must make a determined effort to tap the hidden resources of others. You must think twice before you judge others; you must try to see behind their faces to the real people. A portion of my troubles with the surgeon I wrote about stemmed from the fact that I did not make any attempt to see below the surface of his outward appearance.

I believe that everyone has hidden resources. The tragedy is that so often people do not take the trouble to unearth them. I have seen—again and again in clinic and hospital ward—people called "hopeless" and "misfit," people called "bum" and "no-good" turned into constructive people when someone—often just *one* person—showed a little interest and faith in them. *Just a little interest and faith.*

Inhibition can keep you from reaching your full resources.

A youthful insurance salesman from Texas came to see me a few years ago. He spoke articulately and was a good-looking man, but it soon was obvious to me that he was too cautious and hid the full extent of his ability both from himself and from other people.

He told me about his fright at speaking before groups of other salesmen. He always hesitated to express himself at these meetings—inhibited, he would sit and listen as others talked—but then he was asked to address a large conference of salesmen, to share one of his experiences with them. He stood up to face the audience, he told me, and then he fainted.

"What were you so afraid of?" I asked him.

"I thought I would make a mistake," he said. "Then all the other fellows would lose their respect for me."

I told him that he would still be a good man —even if he did make a mistake (or many mistakes) and that if he could disinhibit himself and unearth his hidden resources he would feel so much richer as a person.

And, I might have added, a person who can think more clearly because he is less frustrated and less fearful and more in command of his reality.

7. Habit of self-discipline

Clear thinking is also disciplined thinking. *Self-discipline* seems to be in discredit today, and yet the undisciplined person does not know where he is going. Discipline, indeed, can make the difference between your potential and your actuality.

You cannot allow a total anarchy of your thoughts. You must set goals through which you channelize your thinking. You must set limits within which you concentrate your powers. You must set boundaries to separate empathy and self-interest. For clear thinking, even though at times latitude and freedom are essential, you still need a framework of self-discipline and you must make a habit of this.

8. Imaginative development of will power

You must use your imagination to develop the kind of will power that will lead you to success and more success.

Go to your closet and get out your motion-picture projector.

Now flash the picture on the screen.

The screen of your mind.

What do you see?

You see success pictures—our features for today: the knockout punch of the leading heavy-weight prize fighter; an actress so involved in her role that she brings tears to your eyes; a politician staking his reputation on a speech in which he takes a bold, affirmative stand; a great pitcher unwinding and firing, striking out his man and winning the ball game. Two double features, four winners.

You must use such imagination to project into your mind success pictures of yourself. To develop your will toward success. To build your power to create success.

You see in your mind, again and again, *your* past successes and *your* good moments.

Properly using your imagination, you build your self-image and pave the way for clear thinking.

9. Nostalgia—for today

Your nostalgia is not for yesterday, but for today. Each day you aim at self-improvement and you aim at improving the clarity of your thinking.

You see the past in proper focus, but you do not live in the past. You use the past to learn from past mistakes, not to escape from the present.

You have lived through heartaches and tragedies; I have, too.

You cannot forget?

Perhaps you cannot.

Still, you can use substitution to forget. You utilize today to concentrate on your goals and then have less time to obsess yourself with the tragedies of yesterday.

Now and then, if you must, walk into a room of yesterday where on the walls you catch glimpses of your old joys and sorrows—but only for a short time.

Then return to today. This is clear, creative thinking.

10. Knowledge of direction

When you strike a golf ball, you know the direction of its flight—I hope you do, anyway.

You must also know the direction of your thinking. If, as a daily goal, you set yourself the task of thinking about your finances, it will do you little good if you get trapped in resentment at your boss, humming TV commercials, and remembering some irrelevant anecdote you heard a few days before.

While writing this book, I took a break and happened onto a television play about a great power blackout—I believe it referred to the one that hit the East a few years ago. It was about a group of people stranded in an office building during blackout conditions and about their often negative attempts to adjust to it.

I write about my own experiences with the power blackout in *Creative Living for Today* (Trident Press, 1967) so I won't describe them again —I live on the eighteenth floor of a building in mid-Manhattan and had some time (without elevator running) getting downstairs to grab a taxi to catch a plane—but this play brought to my mind once again the overwhelming impact of living with darkness—without emotional illumination—and without a sense of direction.

For you must know where you are going.

To think clearly, you must dissolve emotional blackout and focus your sense of direction. This is basic.

Reflection is a key step in achieving direction, and thus in clarifying your thinking. Make use of your spare time to relax and reflect, to line yourself up and put yourself in order, where you are and where you are going. This is time well spent!

11. Integrity

Integrity is the heartbeat of clear thinking. Integrity involves even more than honesty. For honesty can involve only a passive acceptance of what is right and what is wrong, while integrity involves an active seeking out of truth both internally and in relation to other people. The person who has integrity can afford to think clearly, feeling no need to be evasive—with himself or with others. He has no need to waste time sweeping dirt under the rug since he has nothing to hide.

I read an article in my newspaper recently which spoke eloquently of the integrity of an individual, a white baseball executive. This man, executive of a major league baseball club, hired Satchell Paige, the great Negro pitcher whose main days of prowess came before Negroes could play in the major leagues. He hired Paige in his sixties to pitch and in other capacities so that Paige could serve some more major league time (he had pitched in the big leagues for a short time in the twilight of his career) and qualify for a retirement pension. *To pitch—in his sixties!* This transcends even the racial implications, however, and involves simple human integrity: that this executive pursued truth and felt for another human being and insisted on self-respect for a man who as an athlete earned it.

Build integrity in yourself, and you are on the way to clear, creative thinking.

12. New nucleus of faith

Even if it is new—if you have doubted yourself in the past—your belief in yourself will give you confidence. And this will help you to think clearly and creatively.

Build this faith in yourself, but don't expect too much. You cannot expect yourself to build a towering faith in yourself—like a Franklin Roosevelt or a John Kennedy, like a Churchill or an Eisenhower.

Build a new nucleus of faith in yourself that is reasonable in terms of who you are. And a faith in others, too.

On a visit to the West Coast, I delivered a lecture in Spokane, Washington. It was a pleasant experience; I was in a good mood and my audience was appreciative.

Afterward, an attorney came up to the lecture platform and invited me to come with him to his home; he was consulting with four couples who intended to get divorces. They had been among my audience and they were trying to improve themselves; the attorney was trying to save the marriages.

"Certainly," I said. "I hope we can help them."

The attorney's home was comfortable and the conversation may have been a little strained, but there were attempts at communication—or so it seemed to me.

Then one of the husbands went to the bathroom and I overheard his wife say, "Yes, yes, I forgive him, but I cannot forget."

Now, this is no nucleus of faith; it is no form of real forgiveness either. And it is not only no nucleus of faith in her husband; it also indicates a lack in herself to begin with.

What you need is a belief in yourself and in others, too—one that is with a full heart—and this will lead you toward clear thinking, which is in essence a reflection of your ability to find peace of mind.

13. Growth as a human being

All these components of clear thinking mean growth as a human being. In clear thinking, in purposeful doing, you grow and reach out toward self-fulfillment. You reach out toward maturity, security, happiness, and inner peace in an interreactive process which flows to and from clear, rational, creative thinking.

This completes our analysis of the components of clear thinking. We have spelled them out for you; now spell them out for yourselves as they apply to you individually.

YOUR SEARCH FOR FULFILLMENT

Man's search for fulfillment has occupied the minds of thinkers throughout recorded history. Philosophers, social reformers, political manipulators, utopian theorists, economic planners—all manner of men have looked for the solution in various plans involving systems of thinking and orderings of social forces.

I put the emphasis in this great search of yours where I feel it belongs—on you.

On the health and strength of your self-image.

On your ability to think clearly, coherently, and rationally.

In this chapter we have analyzed the nature of clear thinking, factors underlying it and factors contributing to its power and scope.

I believe it will help you to use your thinking power more constructively and to propel you along that superbly paved highway leading to your self-fulfillment.

4

TEN STEPS TOWARD RELAXATION

The search for relaxation is one of the great searches of our time. It is a treasure hunt without end—for we seek relaxation ceaselessly, hungrily, in an age of frantic, disturbed people who have forgotten how to relax. Many people feel this goal—relaxation—is unattainable in these hustle-bustle times, in this oh-so-uncertain world.

Yet this search is such an important one. It is a golden goal that we seek, an inner quiet, an untroubled sea that flows within us, a music of sweet violins and gently tinkling bells—relaxation.

And, as we go about our work, focusing on our major goal of self-fulfillment, we must study the multiple factors that contribute to relaxation. For without relaxation, without inner peace, there can be no self-fulfillment that lasts.

The life process seems to be such that you do not very often get something for nothing. No genie stands at your beck and call waiting to serve you a magic dish called RELAXATION. Far from it. Relaxation is a personal quest, a personal achievement and you must step out and fight for it. It will not come over you because you have a bank account, an automobile, a suntan, a house, a host of servants, an expensive piano, or a pent-house. It will not come over you because you own stocks, or real estate, or a mansion that others envy.

All these elements of material success may be important, and useful, and they may be helpful to you. But they will not automatically bring you relaxation; you must bring yourself relaxation.

In ten steps. I will shortly spell them out for you.

But, first, a few more words about relaxation. Now, it may be true that if you take relaxation and try to put it as a down payment on a house, you may see others looking at you warily, as if they'd like to put you in a cage. And if you take your relaxation and try to deposit it in the bank, you might catch the bank teller motioning the police-man to move a little closer, just in case.

All right, so it's not tangible. But it is none-theless precious.

And its preciousness is alive in a rich inter-active process. You give your relaxation to others and you help them enormously. Others give their relaxation to you and you feel stirrings of gratitude welling within you that make you glad you're alive.

Or the contrary may be true. Suppose you go to a restaurant. You're with friends, and you're all in a good mood. You all sit around a table and the waiter comes over to take your order. He is extremely nervous and fidgety. You feel sympa-thetic and try to make him feel at ease, but still, why does he keep hovering over the table, rushing to rearrange your silverware (you have already arranged it), to refill your glass of water (you've only taken a tiny sip), and to ask why you signaled him (you just happened to glance in his general direction)? In a few minutes, your waiter's lack of relaxation has become contagious; you and your companions gradually get more fidgety and you fidget your way through what might have been a pleasant, relaxing dinner.

I give this, of course, only as an example and my feeling is one of sympathy for anyone who is nervous and harassed in his work—as is this imaginary waiter of mine.

But it is an example of the importance of relaxation, of its infectiousness and power, and of the negative and spreading results when this quality is missing in people.

It is a key stop on the road to self-fulfillment. If you bypass this stop, you will not get to your intended destination.

RELAXATION—FOR YOU

And, now, your ten steps toward relaxation. Let me spell them out for you.

1. **R** Requirements for Relaxation.
2. **E** Enjoyment.
3. **L** Looking for Leisure.
4. **A** Acquiring Goals for Self-fulfillment.
5. **X** X Marks the Spot for Your Inner Revolution.
6. **A** Adventure in Lifelong Youth.
7. **T** Triumph over Tension.
8. **I** Insurance for True Security.
9. **O** Overcoming the Pitfalls of "Tomorrow."
10. **N** Nostalgia for Mental Tone.

We will go up these steps one at a time—no escalator, no quick ten-second digests.

1. Requirements for relaxation

We need certain requirements or techniques for any undertaking; a plan, and a beginning, middle, and ending for the implementation of this plan. If we aim at achieving relaxation, we must first of all set this as our goal.

We must understand what we mean by relaxation; by relaxation I do not mean merely physical relaxation and I do not advocate an attempt to achieve physical relaxation anyway by either sustained effort or intricate diplomacy. In relation to sleep, for example, many people who count sheep stay awake, and others may drink hot milk at bedtime only to find themselves with a gastrointestinal upset.

Your forebrain is the vital area in which you activate your drive toward self-fulfillment through relaxation, but you cannot use your forebrain for willful direction or for forcing the materialization of your goal.

Once you desire it, you move toward relaxation when you use your servo-mechanism in the midbrain that works subconsciously to achieve for you relaxation.

Therefore, in moving toward relaxation, you let your servo-mechanism serve you in *its* way; you do not attempt to force it *your* way.

Realizing this, you will understand that physical activities can prepare you for relaxation without, of necessity, accomplishing it. The execution is subconscious and when this is done you relax in all ways, including physically.

Then you contribute nothing toward your relaxation? Of course you do. You trigger it all off yourself with

- desire to relax
- overcoming negative feelings that block your desire to relax
- building your self-image
- your ability to live with pressure.

2. Enjoyment

Relaxation means enjoyment, which involves an ability to live with happiness without spoiling it and an ability to survive misfortune and bounce back, with the elasticity of a rubber band, to your better self.

The person who can enjoy rises above passivity and feels an excitement when he thinks of new experiences. He is not afraid of newness, and of change. He lives for the moment and turns his back on the past. He encourages relaxation because he encourages joyful living.

The frightened, tense person may give others the power to judge him and find him wanting.

But you, be your own judge, a wise and compassionate judge, and pass a gentle judgment upon yourself:

NOT GUILTY.

Not guilty of being a criminal. Not guilty of being inferior. Not guilty of being an unworthy human being who deserves punishment.

Instead, you see that you are a human being who does not have to reach perfection, who deserves to be happy and to cultivate his capacity for enjoyment—the birthright of all human beings.

Not guilty. Enjoy. Relax.

Let me tell you a story.

A man came to see me. He said he needed help. Would I talk to him? I would.

We sat in my living room and I looked at him. In his middle or late forties, an angry-looking man. He was not enjoying meeting me; he seemed as if he enjoyed little, if anything, in life.

He told me about himself. He was a construction worker and this had been his occupation for many years. He had been one of the men who had helped erect the many new skyscrapers in Manhattan in recent years.

"You have good work," I said. "Good honest work. You are a man who builds."

His face was very serious. "I guess so," he said.

"Have you been doing this a long time?"

His hair was gray, his face tight. "Quite a while."

"Why did you come to see me?"

"I've never liked myself," he said. "I can't stand myself."

"Why?"

"Well, I don't know. But I just don't like myself."

I looked at him. I did not think his over-serious expression was temporary; he looked as if he didn't know what it meant to enjoy something.

How could I help him? I asked him more about himself.

He told me about something that had obsessed him all his life. In school, as a youngster, a teacher had said he was stupid, and that he would never amount to anything. He had never forgotten this teacher's remark, and had adopted this critical attitude toward himself.

After this, he had done poorly in school. He had failed a number of subjects; his grades in others were barely passing. More than once he had been tempted to cheat on exams. He had resisted this urge, but finally had dropped out of school. And ever since, he had considered himself a failure.

In a sense, this was ironical because he had achieved quite a lot since. Getting into the construction industry when help was badly needed, he had held his job for many years. He had been a soldier in the war. And, finally, he had married

—and stayed married—and was in the process of raising five children. His oldest daughter, in college, had been reading my book *Psycho-Cybernetics;* he had borrowed her copy and read it, too. He had liked it and decided to come to see me; maybe I could help him.

"I don't like myself," he repeated. "I haven't liked myself since I was a kid."

"Why not? What do you think is wrong with you?"

"I don't know," he said again. "But I feel angry—and defeated. Sometimes I'm there, way up there, doing my work, and I ask myself why I don't just jump and get it over with."

"And?"

"There's my wife and kids. I can't do it because of them."

"And yourself? Your life? Your self-respect?"

He shrugged his shoulders.

"You want to know what I think?"

He nodded glumly.

"If you want to jump," I said, "don't jump from a skyscraper. Jump from the negative person you feel you are to the successful person you are sometimes."

"Me? Successful?" He looked somber.

"You think that's funny," I said. "Why don't you smile if you think it's funny?"

"Why should I?"

"Because you don't seem to ever smile. At all."

"Doc," he said, "what in hell do I have to smile about?"

"See yourself with some perspective," I said. "You've had failures, but no person alive doesn't feel he's a failure sometimes. I've failed; why shouldn't you? Everyone fails sometimes. But look at your successes. Get away from the past and look at what you've accomplished. All these years working steadily, doing your work. You're an adult, working as an adult, married, with five children. To have five children, growing up, a girl in college —you have supported them with your hard work and watched them grow—and you don't think this is a success?"

It was not much of a smile on his face, but it was a smile. "I never thought of things that way," he said.

"Stop dwelling on your failures," I said. "You've had successes too; think of them. Then you'll be able to smile more and to know what enjoyment is."

"Thanks," he said.

"Keep in touch," I said.

3. Looking for leisure

Looking for leisure is an active and complicated process. You may think it is simple; it is not.

We are not simply work machines. The good worker, the productive person also knows how to seek leisure and how to use it for relaxation.

The person who takes his work with him wherever he goes may not even work well.

For, often, such a person will find himself tied up in knots of tension, blocked off from escape and renewal, carrying his frustrations and fatigues into his work, drowning his powers of concentration in his overflowing pool of trouble.

You're too busy? Too many demands are made on you? It's possible, I'll grant, but I don't really believe this.

Many demands are made on me—I write, I lecture, I practice plastic surgery, I have personal responsibilities—but I find leisure time. I will not tolerate not finding it; I owe it to myself.

You must feel this way, too.

Solitude as a way of life may be self-defeating evasion of responsibility, but small doses of solitude are often therapeutic. You can then, refreshed, return to other people, bringing to them the relaxation you gave yourself with your positive use of your leisure time.

You can use your precious time to find new interests, new goals, new sides of yourself, new sides to your loved ones.

4. Acquiring goals for self-fulfillment

To relax, you must define your goals, recognize your limits, know when it's time to stop working and play a little. If your goals are demanding and intricate, you must develop the ability to sense when it's time to pack in your day's work and find oases of non-demanding peace.

Stop expecting the impossible of yourself! Impossible means just that—not possible. You can only do so much. You're not an army, or a huge corporation; you're just one human being.

Limiting your goals reasonably is very important. You must consider many factors: age, temperament, the strength of your self-image, economic status, and so on. My point is that if you set goals which constantly test the limits of your capacities, you will feel tense and frustrated and chances are your temper will be continually on edge.

When I was a boy, living on New York's crowded Lower East Side, I could run all day and often I did. I would have fun in all our choose-up games of baseball and stickball and all kinds of other games, and I could on summer vacations spend a whole day running and throwing and catching and arguing. These were my goals and I liked them fine.

Would I do this today? Would you, at my age? Of course not.

This is obvious; factors such as age are easily seen as limiting tangible physical activities.

You must learn to be just as sensitive in perceiving other, more subtle limits that you must place on your goals.

Refuse to drive yourself beyond your capacities. Relaxation and pressure just don't go together. At times it is true that, under the stress of external forces, you may be compelled to overextend yourself and even do things you don't like —but that's not a lifetime. You must be resilient, bounce back to yourself, and reach out for new goals.

5. X marks the spot for your inner revolution

This revolution is taking place inside you now, and it is a special kind of revolution—no bloodshed, no violence—a quiet rebirth of your true self.

Probing, you seek to find out who you are. You seek to discover and integrate the best parts of yourself. When you find them, and find them in spite of the turmoil and trouble in our most confused and difficult universe, you will be moving toward relaxation.

In this revolution, you do not take to the streets. You need no sticks or stones. Your aim is not destruction at all; you seek only to construct.

All you really need is a chair. And X marks the spot where you sit in your chair, your Think Chair, which is not a stationary chair. Your Think Chair implies motion—not motion back and forth, back and forth like a rocking chair, but a force more dynamic. Your Think Chair is your launching pad, in which you take off, jet-propelled, on the most exciting adventure of your life, inside yourself to the good within you, and away from yourself to find the good in others, remembering that though you, in your Think Chair, build a strong, proud, independent island within yourself, still you belong on the mainland with your human brothers and sisters. In your creative growth, you aspire and you relax.

Your Think Chair is your Magic Carpet. Having taken a creative and healing look within yourself, you are now able to travel far and wide, with greater insight, into the world of reality.

The brilliant cellist Pablo Casals recently celebrated his 90th birthday. Many people his age would talk gloomily of death or of illness. He talked instead of rebirth, of how each day he was reborn.

You must, too—at your age.

6. Adventure in lifelong youth

You stay young; your age does not matter. This is high adventure, for many people surrender to age, bow before it and fear it more than reality justifies.

But you, even if you are 60 or 65 or older, you refuse to obsess yourself with thoughts of your age. You feel young. You renounce physical activities that your age excludes you from, but your thinking is young. It is new. It is fresh.

You renounce the passive life of many older people. You live actively.

You renounce the yesterday-type thinking of many older people. You live today.

And in this youthfulness you can relax—young or old.

And, if you read these words and are young in age, they can be of value to you today: in thinking of your later years as years of adventure, of excitement, of full living and full participation in the world.

7. Triumph over tension

We are in the jet age. Jets whiz through our skies, bringing California close to New York, Detroit close to Paris, making the entire world a smaller place. This acceleration has many advantages—speaking for myself, I can lecture for several days in Denver, Colorado, and in no time be back in New York to attend to my affairs there; so this speed helps me.

Still the rapid pace seems to have increased our tensions. Look at people around you and you can see the tension: in faces, voices, hands. Internally, invisible to you, this tension may be expressed in terms of spasms of stomach or intestines.

How do we triumph over these tensions?

Muscles tense, contracting without purpose, or more than they should. Your forehead is creased into a frown, your upperlip is raised; you repress a crying spell. The muscles around your eyes may twitch. You may breathe heavily with your chest muscles when you should be breathing from your abdomen. If your mouth is not open, you grit your teeth or bite your lips and overuse the muscles around your chin.

Now, how do we triumph? How do we change this face of tension to one of relaxation?

Awareness of this abuse of your musculature does not necessarily constitute a cure. You must realize that your muscles are working so hard because of disturbances of your mind. Therefore, proceed to the source of the trouble: your mind. And, to do this, suppose you imagine that your mind has a face.

Now keep your imagination alive and see a frown of confusion on the face of your mind. Teeth gritted and jaw firm. Now open your mouth

—in your imagination—and smile slightly. Relaxation will follow because you cannot have a tense face with an open mouth as well as a slight smile.

Carry this further. Unclench your hands. Open them up and unclench them. Feel better?

Now take a little time—even five minutes will help—and talk to yourself:

Tell yourself that God created you to succeed, not to fail, that He made you a unique individual.

Tell yourself that you have more than shortcomings, that you are a worthwhile person, that you have done good things in life.

Remind yourself of your past successes and *see* them again. Close your eyes so you can concentrate to your fullest capacity, and visualize these past successes. Bring them into your mind, and live through them once again until this feeling of success—that you once knew, even if for a few moments—lives again. Remember that you are much more than a failure.

Now, one more thing:

Close your eyes again and see, in your imagination, a geyser. This geyser is blowing off steam. Think of this symbolically. Think of it as release, as symbolic release of tensions, as release of distress, and even if for only a few minutes, let the tensions flow from you like the steam flows from the geyser.

I want to tell you about a woman who won out over her tensions.

She had undergone a severe deprivation; her husband had died. He was no youngster; they were both about sixty. Still, his death had been a great shock. She had loved him, and found that she could not relax.

She had a grown-up daughter—there was solace in this—but still she found time heavy on her hands and tension a constant companion. Money, fortunately, was no worry to her; her husband had left her in a secure position.

But time! What to do with time in which she lived empty and tense.

She decided it was the moment for action. She had to bring life back into her life. And she did this in a simple, realistic way. What could a woman her age do? Well, she could become a babysitter.

She became a babysitter. She was a friendly, companionable person; it suited her personality. Soon she had a substantial clientele; she was in enormous demand. Her telephone was ringing every day; she could not accommodate all the harassed, pressured mothers who needed help.

Spending time with children cheered her. Their cuteness, their joys brought something into her life that made her feel more alive. And then she gave them back good cheer. And, like a volleyball, back and forth went the good cheer and life led to more life.

In her sixties, abandoning the passive concepts of retirement, finding not only balm for her wounds, but using her work to bring her happiness and relief from tension.

She did not find utopia—how could she? But she did the best she could with the reality at hand and, in doing this, won a victory over her inner tensions.

8. Insurance for true security

Most people protect themselves with all kinds of insurance. They protect their lives, their houses, their automobiles, and we have today increasing numbers of complicated and interrelated insurance policies. Many serve their purpose well.

However, if you want true security, and a big

jump toward achieving self-fulfillment, relaxation may be your best insurance policy.

Here are a few suggestions for taking out insurance you need:

A. *Stop fearing failure.* This is negative and will only make you tense. The successful, relaxed person knows he will fail sometimes and takes failure in his stride.

B. *Stop expecting perfection.* You cannot expect perfection—either in yourself, others, or in circumstances. Each day will bring its problems, its conflicts, its defeats. Expect this, and you'll feel better.

C. *Stop selling yourself short.* Remember that you are a human being with dignity, and stop deriding yourself with criticisms that are more worthy of an enemy.

9. Overcoming the pitfalls of "tomorrow"

The relaxed person lives in the present; he does not mope around dreaming of "tomorrow." And, indeed, idle dreaming is not relaxation but evasion that ends up in defeat and tension.

The tomorrow-type thinker, that long-time member of the huge, world-wide Mañana Incorporated, never gets anything done. Days and weeks and months and years float by as he keeps putting things off until tomorrow—and this tomorrow does not come around too often.

We need leisure to better ourselves, to take stock of ourselves, to have fun, to rest up from life's crises—but this has nothing to do with the pitfall of saying to yourself, "I'll do that tomorrow" again and again when what you may really mean is *never*.

Mañana Incorporated—"tomorrow"—it doesn't matter what you call it, it all leads to failure.

Move on your goals, move on them in spite

of conflicts, imperfections, troubles, crises, move on them and *do*.

Even if you fail, you will feel more relaxed because you will know you've done your best.

And if you succeed, well—you may just feel great.

10. Nostalgia for mental tone

An important aspect of relaxation is to yearn for mental, emotional tone—which brings muscle tone to your body. You reach this quality of tone when you are able to free yourself from the dead-weight of negative feelings and dig for the valid treasure inside you.

Archaeologists, resourceful plunderers of time, recently discovered treasures in ancient Greece.

Digging on the east coast of Attica, they discovered fifteen wooden vases carved in geometrical designs—the first discovery of this kind in history. Realizing that fresh air would decompose the wood that had been preserved in fertile mud ever since the fifth and sixth centuries B.C., a noted Greek archaeologist rushed the vases to Athens for a preservative treatment—twenty-three miles away.

Also a professor of an American university found in Greece a Mycenean settlement dating back 3500 years—with temple, palace, private homes with plumbing and a municipal sewer system.

And thus we learn, from time to time, things we never knew about ancient civilizations.

How wonderful it would be if we could dig inside ourselves, expert archaeologists all, and, nostalgic for mental tone, find the treasure inside us.

These treasures are our sincerity, our self-confidence, our capacity for genuine human interrelatedness, our desire to do good and to succeed in our undertakings.

Shovel out?

Ready?

Dig!

Your inner treasures, excavating and developing them; these treasures will bring you a long way toward the achievement of relaxation.

ONE MORE INGREDIENT: FORGIVENESS

Are you a lover of omelets? Scramble up some eggs, cut up some onions, perhaps some cheese or tomatoes . . . Oh, well, you make your omelet, I'll make mine. Besides, maybe I don't want to give you my recipe.

Anyway, and getting back to serious things, we have been discussing a recipe for achieving relaxation in a noisy, turbulent, and insecure age.

But we have left out one ingredient. And, a basic, fundamental one at that.

Forgiveness.

Without forgiveness you will not achieve relaxation. For no matter what success you have achieved, no matter what mountain you have climbed, no matter how much leisure you have, no matter how fine the goals you have delimited, you will still ache from the load of bitterness inside you.

Forgiving is not easy. Someone has wronged you, you feel, and the wrong has hurt you. How can you ever forgive this person?

Let me make two points:

1. *You must try to see things from the other person's point of view*. If you do this, you will see that your point of view may not be completely objective and that your grievance, though painful,

and justified, may not take into consideration alleviating factors which you never considered.

2. *Holding a grudge hurts you most of all.* The person you hate might not even know you're thinking about him. You are the one who suffers from your resentment; you poison yourself with the hostility you will not throw away.

So you see that you must forgive others for hurting you—not only for the feeling of worth and dignity that the act of forgiving will give you —but for your own protection against the damage you will do yourself.

Most of all, however, you must learn to forgive yourself.

You must learn to forgive yourself for your mistakes—past, present, and future. If you never made a mistake, you wouldn't be human. No one would want to know you. You'd be too perfect; no one could feel comfortable with you.

You must learn to forgive yourself for the times you were inconsiderate.

For the times you were not fully responsible.

For the times you were not a good father or mother.

For the times you were not a good son or daughter.

For the times you were not a good brother or sister.

For the times you were not a good friend.

You must forgive yourself for the times your work was not professional.

For the times you were too timid.

For the times you were too bold.

You must forgive yourself for your confusion, for your bad temper, for your bad decisions, for your stupidity and for your stubbornness.

You're not such a bad person, you know. Give yourself the same consideration you'd give a friend and forgive yourself for all your human imperfections. You are a human being, not a god.

When you forgive yourself, you have taken a monumental stride toward relaxation.

LIBERATION AND RELAXATION

A final word about relaxation: you must liberate yourself. You must free yourself.

During the days of the Nazi insanities in Germany and throughout Europe thousands and thousands of innocent victims fled to various sectors of the world to escape. They traveled to Latin America, to other European nations, to the Orient, to the United States.

A middle-aged woman, who had escaped the Nazi terror, came to consult me many years ago. She asked me if plastic surgery could remove the tattoo on her arm: a number, a reminder of grim days. She had lost her family in a concentration camp and, now, safe in America, she had met a man who asked her to marry him. First she wanted the number removed so that she could start a new life. I operated on her and she married her man, a machinist.

Yes, she had been a displaced person, displaced by the Nazi terror. And her loved ones, dead in a concentration camp. But she went on living. She liberated herself from her horrible experiences, liberated herself from the memories of her persecutions, and went on to a new life.

You, too. You must liberate yourself.

You must liberate yourself from negative feelings, from resentment, from fear of failure, from the obsessions with which you torture yourself. You have no Gestapo to root you out, no executioners to flee—still, you must defeat the Gestapo in yourself that would immerse you in a concentration camp you have built for yourself.

You must call on the courage and self-respect within you to overcome these negative feelings so that you can truthfully feel that you are a free person.

A person who can take the ten steps toward relaxation that we have outlined in this chapter, liberates himself.

This is a major move in your search for self-fulfillment.

5

IMAGINATION AND YOUR
SELF-FULFILLMENT

One and one equals two, and two and two equals four. And so on. Mathematics serves our needs for we need precision in life. We must measure things. And exactly. We want to know what time it is. We want to know how much money we have in our savings account. We don't want educated guesses; we want to know.

But everything in life is not so precise, and there is inestimable value in many of our intangibles, which may completely elude mathematical-type analysis.

And so, as we live, plotting our goals, choosing our strategies, planning for survival and dreaming of achieving what is ideal, we turn inward for our help, inward to a force that is invisible, intangible, and yet so very real—to our imagination.

Imagination! You can't bottle it, you can't stuff it into a can, you can't roll it off an assembly line.

Imagination! You can't smoke it, you can't eat it, you can't drink it.

Imagination! You can't see it, you can't hold it in your hand—yet it is there.

The poet William Blake, whose lines still live many years after his death, once wrote this:

To see a World in a grain of sand,
    And a Heaven in a wild flower;
Hold Infinity in the palm of your hand,
    And eternity in an hour.

Blake's undying words express most vividly this power, this precious power—of creative imagination.

Is creative imagination the gift of the few only? Does it belong only to poets, philosophers, artists, and inventors? I don't believe this for one second. For we all have imagination. It is a part of us—like our feet, our arms, our heart, our brain.

Children live in a world that, to a great extent, is make-believe. They make up names for their dolls. They make up new words. They make up new forms of relationships as they play. Reality does not stand in their way—perhaps because they do not know it too well; they turn to their imagination to brighten up their world.

Adults, for realistic reasons, cannot allow such free rein of imagination. For, as adults, it is obvious that we must at all times be in touch with our responsibilities and be prepared to meet the demands that others will make on us. Living in frenetic days of automation and conformity, channelizing our days into routines and rigid patterns, we may feel necessity demands that we starve the free workings of our imagination.

Yet you must hold on to your capacity for using your imagination. You must use this capacity intelligently: to broaden your horizons, to exercise your originality and your uniqueness, and to formulate and oversee the successful attainment of your goals.

Creative imagination is an essential attribute of the successful individual. And you don't have to be an Edison or a Shakespeare or an Einstein. You are a human being, just as are the acknowledged great of our world, and you have a capacity for imagination, too.

It may be neglected; it may be hidden; it may be forgotten—but it is there.

Imagination means the growth of images in your mind, images which you can manufacture for your own welfare. If you build in your mind good, healthy success images—and make a daily task of this—you will be on your way to building a wonderful image of yourself. An image that you can relish.

Using your imagination is a satisfying full-time job. It doesn't end when you leave your office or your store or your factory. No, sir. Imagination stays with you; it is a part of you—like the blood pouring through you, like your heartbeat. And, indeed, imagination is the heartbeat of fulfillment.

Creative imagination belongs to everybody who wants it: rich or poor, child or adult, executive or clerk. All of us, in living creatively, turn to our imagination to work out new answers to old problems.

And now suppose that we study the components of imagination in greater detail.

THE INGREDIENTS OF IMAGINATION

Here they are, spelled out, the ingredients of your imagination:

1. **I**   Inquiring Mind.
2. **M** Motivation.
3. **A**   Action.
4. **G** Goal Setting.
5. **I**   Inspiration.
6. **N** Navigation.
7. **A**   Achievement.
8. **T**   Truth about Yourself.
9. **I**   Intent to Improve.
10. **O** Orientation for Progress.
11. **N** Nucleus of Desire.

Good enough. That spells it out for you. I-M-A-G-I-N-A-T-I-O-N.

So let's go.

1. Inquiring mind

This is basic to any thorough consideration of creative imagination. You inquire about yourself, about others, about things, about your world. You feel a healthy sort of curiosity, which arises out of your deep sense of liveness, out of your interest in your surroundings, out of your involvement in life itself. You refuse to fall into the boredom that besets many people. Your courage reinforces your tendency toward curiosity because you will not, in fright, retreat from the demanding need to keep your eyes open.

You seek truth and knowledge; you wish to get at the heart of things. You are an investigator, a private eye; you are a modern detective solving the problems of modern living.

Let me tell you a story: It is about Dr. Bell, a tall, slender man with bushy hair, white face and long nervous fingers. See him now, in his lecture room at Edinburgh University, surrounded by young men as he examines the case load that the morning brings.

Patient number one. Dr. Bell's shrewd Scottish

eyes survey him quickly. "Gentlemen, who do we have here? A cobbler? I believe so. And a first-class cobbler, I would say, for he looks as if he's been busy indeed. Well, my good fellow! Are you not a busy *left-handed* cobbler?"

The patient is bewildered; to his knowledge, Dr. Bell has not seen him before. How could he describe him with such exactness, then?

The cobbler's condition diagnosed, Dr. Bell turns swiftly to the next patient. He studies him for just a few minutes:

"An old soldier, right? Service in India, I believe—Afghan border? That's a nasty wound in your leg. Sit down and relax; get the weight off it. We will see what we can do to help you."

He was not infallible, the great Dr. Bell, but he was close to it, and some of his students thought him a magician.

And what constituted his magic?

"Observation," Dr. Bell would explain. "That's all there is to it. Observation."

But the students had been observing—or so they thought—and none of them had identified the first patient as a cobbler.

"Simple, indeed, gentlemen. Did you note the worn places on the man's trousers? Surely they gave away his trade instantly. And, since they were more scuffed up on the right side than on the left side, he was obviously left-handed.

"As for the soldier, his military posture gave him away. The color of his skin indicated service in India. The limp indicated an injury that must have been suffered ten years ago; the only action in India ten years ago took place at the Afghanistan border."

Simple, yes—once you listened to the explanations. Simple, indeed.

The spirit of the brilliant Sherlock Holmes

hovered over this Edinburgh classroom. For a medical student listened carefully to Dr. Bell as he lectured in the 1870's—and remembered well what he heard. He was a tall, shrewd young man. Arthur Conan Doyle.

Detective stories have been popular quite a while; who-done-its not only claim their share of readers, but we also find many detective stories on television. Many of us enjoy the cleverness of the detective, identifying with him, the modern Sherlock Holmes, as he unravels a complicated problem.

And, since it is exciting to play detective, it is certainly fortunate that we can all be Sherlock Holmeses in our own right. By using our imagination. By using our mind to inquire into things.

Be a detective; use your inquiring mind. Your problem: trying to unravel your endlessly, unbelievably complex personality.

See if you can find out why you like some people, yet hate others. Borrow Sherlock Holmes' magnifying glass and focus it on yourself, investigating yourself. See if you can track down your internal enemy Mr. Shortcomings, that part of yourself who fears failure. See if you can track down Mr. Shortcomings, who criminally shortchanges you even though you think he is with you. See if you can bring him out into the open and dispose of him so that you can be a freer person.

You have one wonderful advantage if you play detective to yourself—no other detective has this advantage. Other detectives—Sherlock Holmes, Nero Wolfe, or whomever—use their ingenuity to track down evil. But when you become your own Sherlock Holmes, you are out to track down not only evil, but also to bring out the good qualities in you.

And, when you discover these qualities, you are a great detective. You are discovering something wonderful, qualities to build your self-image on, qualities that will lead you back to your past successes, then forward to new successes.

2. Motivation

Imagination, as we look at it, means motivation to improve yourself. For, chances are that you can plan useful goals in your imagination—and then see their materialization in reality—if your motivation is sound.

In other words, you must want to succeed. You must want the good life for yourself. You must want to build an imagination full of success images. You must want to tear out of your imagination the negative images that are forerunners of failure.

You must motivate yourself. *You* must feel that you are a worthwhile person. And you must have a genuine stake in building your strength—in your imagination, where kings are beggars and beggars are kings.

3. Action

Imagination implies action. Imagination never is passive. Dynamic, kinetic, it changes constantly with the daily need to adjust to circumstances, internal and external, and with the daily need to move toward relaxation and happiness.

You do not exercise your imagination and let it go at that. Your imagination is more than a resting place for the storage and oiling up of your thoughts and images. Positive thinking is wonderful, but you prepare yourself to move one step further—to *positive doing*. You oil your servomechanism and proceed to accelerate its motor so that you can charge forward to your goals.

A great actor like Laurence Olivier is playing the role of Hamlet. He is not Hamlet. You know this; he knows this. And yet he acts as if he is Hamlet, and you suspend your disbelief and you believe he is Hamlet. He projects Hamlet across the footlights, and you accept him as Hamlet.

You, too, can make the connection between imagination and action. Every day you are an actor—we all are—and you can do more than strengthen your imagination with healthy images and inquiring thought. You can do this by carrying out into action the healthy side of your imagination—your success images, not your failure images—and making yourself, in action, the successful person you want to be, not the failure person you want to forget.

Use your imagination positively.

Make this your daily goal.

Build in your imagination images of yourself—in success. Success, past, present, and future. Build these good images every day.

But, then, do more than this. Carry the full power of your imaginative resources back out into the world of reality. If you can supplement the workings of a creative imagination with a capacity for intelligent, purposeful action, you are on your way.

4. Goal setting

Creative imagination means goals. Through imagination goals begin to take shape. Imagination generates the growth of desire which is in effect the take-off point of a goal.

Perhaps you feel you do not have this desire, that you are incapable of formulating definite goals, that you just don't care.

But this is basically not true. No matter who you are, no matter what your circumstances, you feel somewhere the desire to live and be happy.

Set your goals. Start with these universal goals, then move on to other simple, basic goals, then up the ladder to more complex goals.

Use your imagination to help you in your goal setting; see in your mind the goals that, realistically, aside from fantasy, will make you happy.

5. Inspiration

Imagination also implies inspiration. You must learn to use your imaging powers in worthwhile ways that will give your life new meaning.

You may find inspiration in different ways. What inspires one person may depress someone else. And, of course, vice versa.

Sometimes I find inspiration by closing my eyes and bringing into my imagination a mental picture of my father.

As I mentioned earlier, my father died a number of years ago. He died in a horrible accident. But I don't want to write about that here; I want to write about how I bring him to life in my mind.

I close my eyes and I see him again—as real as if I'd last seen him yesterday. Broad-shouldered, erect, with piercing eyes, and a huge, sweeping mustache which he trimmed regularly. He had come to this country as a poor immigrant from Austria, and perhaps this explains why he dressed so immaculately—in richly made suit, silk shirt, with high starched collar and lavish accessories.

I see him again in my mind—though gone, still he lives there—and it inspires me.

Not just his physical image, but the kind of person he was.

I bring back into my mind something that happened when I was younger, the kind of incident that made me proud he was my father.

But before I relate this story, let me give you a little background.

My Dad was kind of a neighborhood arbitrator. He loved to help people settle their arguments, make up their differences; he loved to help people cast off their negations and go on to better things. He claimed that this helped him forget all about his rheumatism, from which he suffered for some time.

Anyway, one day Dad saved a neighborhood boy from cruel punishment. The boy, Tony, was fleeing from another youth named Whitey, a terror to many. Whitey had said that he was going to get Tony, that he was going to slash a knife across his cheek. My Dad learned this as he sat on a pier overlooking New York's East River, enjoying the scenery. Tony, running, stopped to tell him about it urgently.

"Whitey's coming for me now!" gasped Tony.

My father told him not to worry, and showed him where to hide. He would take care of Whitey.

And there was Whitey, looking for Tony.

Dad hailed him in a companionable way and asked if he knew Tony.

Whitey said yes.

"I think Tony will make a fine fabric designer," said Dad. "I'm going to give him lessons in my shop. And maybe you, too, Whitey. There might be something you'd be interested in." Dad got to his feet. "Of course," he added, "if something happened to Tony, I'd be very unhappy." He slapped Whitey on the back in his hearty, friendly way.

There was no trouble. And, I'm sure Dad's rheumatism was better that night.

Dad was always doing this kind of thing, making the community a better place to live in, and making me very proud that I was his son, determined that I would always justify his faith in me.

Anyway, to get back to my main point, when I get depressed, when I'm down on myself, when I need an emotional lift, sometimes I just close my eyes and use my imagination: I see my father again, in his dandyish clothes, with his broad shoulders, with his unswerving eyes above his starched collar and I remember his determination to be a good husband, a good father, a good neighbor, and how he used to extend a helping hand in times of stress.

Sometimes this makes me sad—but it gives me inspiration.

Your imagination can give you inspiration, too. I cannot tell you how—this is so individual—but chances are it can.

6. Navigation

Imagination also means navigation. A modern-day Columbus, you sail in your imagination through the choppy seas of frustration toward new horizons, toward a new port, toward a new self-image.

As you make your voyage through the vast spaces within your mind, finding that the world within you is not flat with emptiness and despair, you, like Columbus, learn that the world within your mind is indeed round—round so that the outreaching hands of success and happiness can encircle it.

Searching within your imagination, you learn that you can improve yourself by overthrowing the tyranny of your old destructive feelings as you look within yourself for the creation of new positive feelings.

7. Achievement

With your imagination you launch yourself toward achievement. You remove the debris of hurt feelings that deprive you of an inner security you deserve.

With your keys you may be able to unlock the front door—of your home and your office—and you may be able to unlock your automobile, too.

Still, your key to relaxation and contentment —and to the satisfactions of achievement—you will find in your imagination.

It is a tragedy when you use your imagination not for achievement, but for your own self-destruction.

As in the case of a man who visited me recently to tell me of his troubles and to see if I could help him.

This poor man's imagination was a beehive of trouble: he saw visions of disaster. He achieved little; his imagination betrayed him.

He was about forty, unmarried, worked for his brother in a store; he wanted to get married and improve himself, but felt too unworthy.

And in his mind he manufactured trouble. Whenever he saw a hearse passing in the street, he had to rush and wash his hands. Whenever he passed a hospital and saw an ambulance, he had to rush and wash his hands. (He lived near a hospital, so this caused him considerable hand-washing.) If he did not wash his hands at such times, he told himself, he would die.

He talked to me of these terrible fears that lived in his imagination and of the frightening ideas his imagination perpetuated. "If I don't wash my hands, I'll be trapped," he said over and over. "I'll be trapped if I don't wash my hands."

In many ways he was a most reasonable person, it seemed to me, but then he would lose himself in these dreadful fears.

How to help him? He had seen a psychiatrist; whether this had helped him or not I did not know. I wanted to do whatever I could to help him to use his imagination for achievement, not for self-destruction.

"What kind of parents did you have?" I asked him.

"They were good religious people. But my mother didn't love my father."

"How do you know that?"

"She didn't like to spend time with him. She would give me a lot of attention so she could avoid him."

We talked further. I could sense that he probably felt guilty over his mother's fussing over him—her overprotective attitude—and doubtless he felt resentment toward both his parents. In washing his hands over and over, perhaps he was symbolically washing away his guilt.

Anyway, what could I tell him to help him to put his imagination to positive instead of negative use—in the interests of achievement?

I said something like this: "Perhaps you need more help than I can give you—if so, go get it. But listen to what I have to say; maybe it will help you.

"Whatever has happened to you in the past is not your fault; you have no need to feel guilty. If your mother and father did not love each other, yours is not the guilt. I know that your life has not been easy—your brother is married and he's your boss, your sister is married too, you feel like the unworthy one in the family.

"You've got to try to keep fighting these dreadful fears. You've got to live in the present and set goals every day and wake up in the morning and try to set goals and fight off your fears.

"I know this won't be easy for you, but you have to keep trying and keep setting goals and keep trying to use your imagination constructively —to reach your goals.

"Remember that your life belongs to you. Keep trying. If my ideas don't help you, maybe somebody else can help you. But try and keep trying. Whatever successes you have had in your life, keep them in your imagination. See them again and again. So you can make something good of your life.

"And good luck! I hope you find yourself."

I don't know what has happened to this man —in truth, I felt the construction worker had more hope since his background was more success-filled and he was more functional, but perhaps I was able to help steer him on the road to using his imagination for achievement and not negation. I hope so.

Anyway, his unfortunate use of his imagination—as a breeding-ground for disaster—this is what you must avoid. You must use your imagination for achievement.

8. Truth about yourself

Creative imagination also implies that you seek the truth about yourself. In the midst of honking automobiles and blaring radios, breathing in air of a quality you might not like to think about and barraged on all sides by television commercials, you turn to your imagination to find a focus. You seek to look into yourself as you are—objectively. You look behind you, before you, and within you.

In your imagination you seek to take stock of yourself—your assets as well as your liabilities.

It is good if you concentrate on overcoming your faults, but this is not enough: You must also give your attention to the development of your assets. You must cherish these assets, and work with them as you keep reactivating the all-important functioning of your success mechanism.

It is also important that you see the past in proper perspective. If you can do this, you can see again your past mistakes, and be in a position to avoid them. I do not mean that you should brood about these past mistakes and blame yourself for them. The real purpose of seeing the past in proper perspective is that you can live today.

Finally, in your imagination you must plan for today. You must see in your mind some of today's possibilities. Your main focus should not be on outcompeting Joe or Harry or Fred; these goals do not carry you to your full potential. Your primary excitement should be to improve yourself, to compete with yourself. You aim at becoming a more mature, complete individual day by day and week by week and year by year.

9. Intent to improve

Let us carry this over a little from the last paragraph. In your imagination you must continue to develop your positive intentions and you must aim them basically at your own improvement, not someone else's humiliation.

What is your intent? Is your intent to imitate other people or to improve yourself, in your own image?

Remember this: You cannot truly succeed if you carry in your mind someone else's image. You must develop your own; as you do, you develop a real confidence in yourself.

The money players in our athletic world forget their failures and think of their successes.

You do this, too, but *your* successes, in your own image. Your aim is your improvement, and you launch this program from the powerhouse within you—your imagination.

10. Orientation for progress

Imagination—creative imagination—means that you know who you are and where you are and what you are doing. You avoid filling your imagination with the poison that stems from obsessive thoughts of failure. You work to reject from your imagination pictures of fear and anxiety; you stop agonizing over endless possible catastrophes and concentrate on building a realistic estimate of the possibilities you face.

After you have set realistic and exciting goals, you analyze in your imagination your human rights. You tell yourself that you have a right to achieve these goals. You tell yourself—that you have as many rights as anybody. You stop downgrading yourself. You are as good as anybody; believe this.

Stop expecting perfection of yourself. If you expect perfection, your orientation is not for progress, but for negation. Because if you expect of yourself what you cannot—what *nobody* can—deliver, what can you expect but failure? God made you to be an individual, a unique person on this earth, but *not* a form of perfection.

See your successes—again and again. Bring your success feelings back and savor them in your imagination. If you eat a tasty slice of sirloin steak, perhaps you keep it in your mouth a few extra seconds so you can savor the deliciousness of this steak. Let it be so with the success images you revive in your imagination: savor them, too. They, too, are delicious.

If your successes have been few, make them last—in your imagination, where they really count.

This is an orientation for progress; it can work. Make it work!

11. Nucleus of desire

A few words on your nucleus of desire, with which you harness the constructive powers in your mind. For, when you carry inside you, when you manufacture inside you, a real desire to succeed and to achieve and to do well—and when you keep this hope alive in your imagination—you are on your way.

You must keep this positive desire alive—in rainy and in sunny weather. Some days you will feel that every frustration is bedeviling you at once —external frustrations that you try to combat, but which you cannot control—and you may be right.

Still, even on these bad days, you must work to keep your desire for the good alive in your imagination.

And, then, tomorrow is a new day.

THE POWER OF YOUR IMAGINATION

I hope I have been able to convey to you the enormous power in your imagination.

The potency in your images is staggering. Read some of the more morbid and terrifying works of Edgar Allan Poe or Franz Kafka—they were masterful and intensely creative writers who have created worlds of magical horror with their superb genius for eerie imagery.

You might, perhaps, enjoy reading Kafka or Poe—if only for the comfort of returning to a more reassuring world, imperfect as it is. But surely to project your imagination in such fashion into life itself is disaster. For your images pack awesome power.

And if you carry in your imagination pictures of horror, of catastrophe, if you see in your imagination fellow humans who are really monsters—your chances for self-fulfillment are slim indeed.

You have read this chapter, thoroughly and thoughtfully. You have digested its contents; you have lived with it a while.

And, surely, you must by this time understand—at least to some degree—the enormous power you can build up in this great intangible of yours, your imagination.

You can use this power for good or for bad. You can fill your imagination with anticipations of pleasure or with forebodings of catastrophe. And your use of your imagination will to a large extent determine whether you move yourself toward pleasure or plunge yourself back into disaster.

As with poet William Blake, you must learn to see "Heaven in a wild flower."

You must learn to see the good and the successful in yourself.

The power of your imagination is your supreme force.

I hope that each and every one of you, my readers, will use this power in a constructive way.

6

SELF-ACCEPTANCE AND
SELF-FULFILLMENT

We continue in our search for self-fulfillment.
This will be a never-ending search; in it we carry
forward the purpose of our lives.

Perhaps you will fail to achieve some of your
goals: you may not be able to earn income in five
figures; you may never buy a new Cadillac; you
may never take a cruise around the world.

Well, may I say this: I hope that you achieve
all the goals which are meaningful for you, but
still, you are in good shape if many fall through
but you attain your main goal—a peaceful sense
of self-fulfillment.

Now we will consider one of the great invisible, intangible, untouchable—yet all-important
—aspects of self-fulfillment.

Self-acceptance.

How important it is to be able to accept yourself!

For, in the final analysis, who is the more
fortunate individual—the one who makes millions
of dollars, circles the globe climbing mountains
and going on safaris, owns estates in half a dozen
different countries, and hates himself, or the one

who quietly works at his humble job, unacclaimed and financially unrewarded, who nevertheless accepts himself for what he is?

The answer is obvious.

Every day, as you go around this confused world in which so many false values may infect you if you are vulnerable, you must remind yourself that you must accept yourself as you are.

Stop downgrading yourself. So what if you're not a movie star. So what if you're not a member of the Jet Set! Stop expecting yourself to live up to goals that are fantasy; come back down to earth and live a little.

Remember this, and remember this every day: You will never be happy if you spend your life trying to be someone else. God created you as a unique individual. You have within you an authentic greatness all your own. Use it; don't waste it! You waste it when you try to be someone else for the simple reason that you are *not* someone else.

Tell yourself to accept yourself every day. Even as the anxieties and the pressures of the day billow around you, tell yourself this—take a few minutes off to remind yourself to accept yourself and you will go back to your pressing responsibilities feeling refreshed.

You move toward self-acceptance when you feel big enough to make peace with your human failings without hiding behind deception and rationalization. Come out of hiding; you are not a criminal. You are an imperfect human being; all your life you will make mistakes—perhaps every day of your life. Mistake-making does not make you a criminal who must hide and appear in public only in some form of masquerade which is a lessening of yourself.

Our aim is to move toward self-acceptance, and we will spell out once again.

YOUR GUIDE TO SELF-ACCEPTANCE

This, then, is your guide to self-acceptance. Study it carefully.

1. **S** Search for the Better You.
2. **E** Enterprise.
3. **L** Longing for Growth.
4. **F** Fact versus Fantasy.
5. **A** Aspiration Autonomous.
6. **C** Courageous Struggle.
7. **C** Compassionate Attitude.
8. **E** Expectation of Miracles.
9. **P** Preparation for Pleasure.
10. **T** Truth-Seeking.
11. **A** Active Awareness.
12. **N** Nucleus of Affirmation.
13. **C** Concentration Plus.
14. **E** Enthusiastic Effort.

Self-acceptance. This is what we're after. Now, how do we take aim on its achievement?

1. Search for the better you

You wake up in the morning and, if you're human, perhaps you'll grumble and grouch around for a few minutes.

Then you look in the mirror as you powder your nose or shave, but what do you see? Someone you like? Someone you dislike? This is so vital. Are you searching for a better you? Do you want to find, and build, a better you? Or are you looking at yourself in your mirror superficially, unthinking, not even dreaming that you are a richer personality than you think you are, not even dreaming that it is possible to better yourself, not even dreaming of the you that could be?

You seat yourself to eat breakfast. Your eyes are wide open now (you were squinting at yourself in the mirror) and you begin to read your morning newspaper. But, as you read it, as you quickly survey what's going on in the world, how about making another quick survey—of the world inside you? What is the news from your world? Let us hope it is better than what you read in your paper —surely there are fewer wars, more positive negotiation, less intense work stoppages, and no strikes against yourself. Anyway, write a good newspaper about yourself. Write a better one every day as you search for a better you.

Did it ever occur to you that there is real greatness in you?

Did it ever occur to you that this greatness awaits recognition—from you?

Did it ever occur to you that you are your most important human being and that the famous people you read about in your newspaper are of no consequence compared to your importance to yourself?

And, did it ever occur to you that in your uniqueness as a human being you have an uncommon potential, which you owe it to yourself to nurture, accepting yourself for what you are, refusing to model yourself on other people?

Keep searching for the better you. Accept yourself as you are and yet, at the same time, keep building on this actuality and making more satisfying this reality. Help yourself.

Everybody sometimes needs help from someone. Even Aristotle got it—from Alexander the Great who, in the hectic days of his military victories, found time to collect specimens of a wide variety of nature life and dispatch them to his philosopher friend for his study. And this was instrumental in helping Aristotle to become the founder of natural science.

You, you must recognize yourself and help yourself. You must help yourself to become the person you want to be.

2. Enterprise

This search, this search for the better you is your greatest enterprise. It is an adventure in creative self-acceptance. No segment of your life can exceed this in significance.

Enterprise is your creative effort to solve the enigma of you. You try to understand and rise above your complexities and problems. You work to improve yourself. You ask yourself—

Why do I keep worrying about things that never—or very seldom—happen?

Why do I keep telling myself I am a failure because I failed once or twice—or a few dozen times—in the midst of my successes?

Why do I force my opinions on others when I know this will lead only to resentment?

Why do I hold a grudge about something that happened years ago when this will only hurt me?

With enterprise you do battle to the negative feelings that would belittle you and destroy your true identity.

With enterprise you increase the strength of your personality as you seek to find new horizons and to more fully accept the horizons you have already discovered.

With enterprise you move forward into the world as a dynamic force.

Enterprise means that you are the president of a company—*you*. You are a V.I.P., Chairman of the Board, your vote is decisive, your wealth staggers the imagination, you are a growth company whose price-earnings ratio is conservative no matter what the figures, as you build your structure of unique resourcefulness.

Too many people spend the precious days of their lives "Waiting for Godot," like the characters in the play by Samuel Beckett. They place themselves in positions of helpless passivity, waiting, waiting, waiting, for something that never comes. They look for someone else to come help them, when they must take the initiative and help themselves. Then, like Beckett's frustrated people, they punish themselves and punish others and endlessly recite their complaints and tales of woe. And, of course, they never find what they seek—nor do they really look.

What they need—what you need—is enterprise.

3. Longing for growth

As you accept yourself for what you are, you free your capacity for growth. Since you will accept yourself as you are, you will accept yourself if you fail; therefore, you can move toward growth without fear.

You long for growth, and this is a wonderful desire. It is unfortunate that so many adults have renounced this desire and have settled back instead into a form of inertia which is a tragedy because when they were small children chances are it was alive.

Close your eyes now, turn on the motion picture projector in your mind, and see a baby. For here is longing for growth in action. The baby reaches out. It reaches out to grow—through touching, seeing, probing, tasting, hitting, tearing apart. The baby investigates its little world with all the curiosity of a Newton, a Pasteur, a Galileo. The baby's experimentations never stop.

Now, how about you?

You, too, owe it to yourself to explore your world. You must take out your compass; you must create latitude and longitude for yourself; you must be your own pilot and your own navigator. Your destination? New Islands. New islands of belief in yourself. New routes to peace of mind. New fortresses within which you can nourish the seeds of your increasing self-acceptance.

In accepting this longing for growth, you also accept the world of dangers. You renounce womb-like living in which you can never get hurt but can never find satisfaction because you will never take a chance.

Still, you seek to minimize and control the dangers and to focus on the positive goals and straightforward means of attaining them.

You cannot over-limit yourself. True, you must acknowledge reasonable limitations, but this is different from over-limiting yourself. When you over-limit yourself, you allow fear to take over your body and soul and you block yourself off from growth.

Over-limitation carries with it a narrowness of perspective resulting in a grave tumor of doubt that obstructs your vision and keeps you from realizing your own worth as a human being. You then surrender to loneliness that separates you both from yourself and from others, and, constricting your personality, you impose a jail sentence on yourself—often a sentence for life.

Reflect upon this very seriously. You are not a criminal, you have committed no punishable offense against society—and yet *you* may have imprisoned yourself.

Without even a lawyer to defend you.

Without a jury trial.

With only one extremely severe and unfair judge in attendance.

You.

You are free only when you accept yourself as you are, yet extend yourself outward into life seeking growth, refusing to let negative feelings plunge you into a bleak penitentiary in your mind.

4. Fact versus fantasy

You must learn how to differentiate between fact and fantasy; this is basic to any form of healthy living. Your communication with yourself must be real. If you keep mulling over and over in your mind some mistake or some misfortune of the past, you are living in a dream world of fantasy—not in reality. It is when you forget your grievances of the past and live in the present that you begin to live in the world of fact.

The renowned Italian dramatist Luigi Pirandello wrote a play called *Six Characters in Search of an Author*. These characters were searching for the author to find their identity.

Now, psycho-cybernetically speaking, you are the author in search of six characters—all you. You seek happiness, unhappiness, confidence, frustration, success, failure. All six of you—but which roles do you choose to play?

Happiness? Or unhappiness?

Confidence? Or frustration?

Success? Or failure?

You are the author. You are the director. You can instruct the actor. You can rewrite the script and remold the actor. As you do this, you steer yourself toward fact or toward fantasy; you strengthen or weaken your self-image. *You* do this.

With self-acceptance you choose reality and with it the roles of happiness, confidence, and success. With self-acceptance you no longer need the unreal world of fantasy. Because the way you are is all right with you.

Pirandello also wrote *You Are What You Think You Are*, in which he differentiates between reality and illusion. This is such an important distinction; you must at all times be as aware of this distinction as you possibly can.

Are you living through prestige symbols, striving to keep up with others in fantasy? Then you are not living your own life.

You function at your best when you accept yourself so well that you will not let your mistakes and imperfections drive you fearfully into a make-believe world.

5. Aspiration autonomous

One of the basic aspects of self-acceptance is aspiration, in that you believe in yourself and strive to transform your belief into creative performance. In aspiration you move toward your goals, creatively, and you pursue opportunity wherever you find it.

Aspiration means that you accept yourself not in a passive, but in an active, sense. You know yourself as a goal striver and you know happiness, you feel happiness, as reaching your goals.

Your emotional antennae, your own radar system, you must use to pierce the clouds of frustration blocking off the sunshine in your mind. Your own astronaut, you explore the inner space in your mind and launch your capsule out toward the wonderful world of self-fulfillment.

Your safety valve, your controlling valve, is your degree of self-acceptance. Your self-acceptance enables you to put a bolstering floor under you to protect you from misadventures and failures. If you accept yourself, you cannot lose.

Recently I attended a meeting of Alcoholics Anonymous on the West Coast and I listened to a doctor, a member, talk about the development of alcoholism in an individual—from occasional drinks to heavy drinking to blackouts and remorse.

We can organize, too. Suppose that we call our organization Aspiration Autonomous, and here are our rules:

A. An island within yourself, you are autonomous.

B. You turn your back on negative feelings; you will not allow them to destroy your faith in yourself.

C. You concentrate on positive goals; you set your goals, then you move to achieve them.

D. In your autonomy, though you are an island within yourself, still you stay on the mainland with other people and share your self-respect with them.

6. Courageous struggle

You accept life as it is and, just as you accept yourself with your many imperfections, you also work to accept the world with its many imperfections. You are realistic, but you do not despair.

I am fortunate in that my father taught me the meaning of courageous struggle. He came to this nation from Austria, an impoverished young man, and he worked hard, courageous, struggling, to make money in his work—fabrics. He led a life that was a model of courage. He did not upbraid himself when he made mistakes and he did not surrender to despair. He would not buckle under to bullies; he would even protect neighbors from bullying.

Courage goes with self-acceptance as ham goes with eggs. And I do not believe you can feel true self-acceptance if you do not have the capacity to struggle courageously for your rights.

7. Compassionate attitude

A compassionate attitude is almost synonymous with self-acceptance. For it is not enough, not nearly enough, to be compassionate toward others; compassion must start with yourself.

If you do not forgive yourself—for your mistakes and for your human feelings—you obviously cannot accept yourself.

There is much talk about alienation these days and we hear again and again about "alienated" individuals and about an "alienation" toward the organization of society. But what about the individual's alienation from himself? This is what is fundamental.

No matter what the circumstances, you must refuse to allow yourself to be alienated from yourself. You must accept yourself come what may.

You must accept yourself in sunshine, rain, snow, hail, or sleet.

You must accept yourself in riches, poverty, as creditor or debtor.

You must accept yourself—and feel compassion for yourself—when you talk in a group with fluency and intelligence or when in a group you are tongue-tied and incoherent.

Your compassion for yourself must extend to all situations, to all characteristics, to all possible contingencies.

Any good friend will give you the benefit of a compassionate attitude when you need it from him. The least you can do is give this same compassion to yourself.

Earlier, I wrote about one of my bad days. Let me tell you about another bad day:

It was raining when I woke up, grumpy, and first off I cut myself shaving. Grimly, I bandaged my chin.

Dressing, I groped for my goals; since I hadn't slept as well as I usually did, my thinking wasn't too clear. Ah, yes. An operation in the morning. A conference with my publisher in the afternoon. In the evening I would work on my next book.

Okay, I was finally rolling. Or was I? As I was buttoning my shirt, a button came off in my hands.

A small thing, to be sure, but in the mirror I noticed that the bandaid hadn't stopped the bleeding on my chin.

Breakfast was not too pleasant. The morning newspaper headlined unsettling news, it was the first of the month, which brought a pile of bills.

Then a relative phoned. Illness in the family.

Now, what did I do with my day?

I did what I always do on bad days. I reformulated my goals. Maybe I would not make new friends this day, maybe I would not be as considerate or tactful as on days when I felt better, maybe I would not be as productive, but I would reach some goals.

A. I would perform my operation—efficiently, successfully.

B. I would confer with my publisher. I would make my points; I would listen to his. This would concretize my thinking on the book I was writing.

C. No more goals. The other goal, to work on my book, no. Tomorrow. (This was not *mañana* type thinking. I had to recognize my limitations on this day. I was not up to par.)

And I accepted myself—with compassion.

I felt compassion for myself—even though I was not at my best.

You, too, must give yourself compassion.

8. Expectation of miracles

Recently I drove from Salinas, California to San Jose approximately fifty miles away to speak one Sunday morning at a church. Time was running short and we didn't know the road too well; *only a miracle will get me there on time,* I said to myself.

One minute before the services started, I walked into the minister's office and we both sighed in relief. Behind his chair I saw a sign—It read, EXPECT A MIRACLE.

All of us occasionally suffer from feelings of frustration and despair and feel that we are unlucky, that we just cannot get a break in life. I do not believe there is anybody who doesn't once in a while feel this way. And, at such times, all of us can use a miracle—or the expectation of a miracle.

And you have every right to expect a miracle . . . every right to believe that a miracle is forthcoming.

But not in a literal sense, of course. No one can literally expect miraculous intervention in his behalf.

Your miracle must come from inside yourself. It must come from your faith in yourself no matter how trying the pressures. It must come from your attitude of determination in crises, as you turn crises into creative opportunities. It must come from the support you give yourself under all circumstances.

The real miracle you can, and must, expect then is your self-acceptance.

Your acceptance of your weakness.

Your acceptance of your strength.

Your acceptance of your imperfections.

Once you accept yourself, you can give yourself help that is little short of miraculous.

9. Preparation for pleasure ·

Each day you prepare yourself for pleasure. This is a key element in self-acceptance because it is no easy task to accept yourself when you are continually undermining yourself and setting yourself up for defeat and depression.

A young child is building with blocks, and you close your eyes again and see him in your mind. The image of this child builds in your imagination—focus this image—and you see him on his hands and knees, placing one block on top of another, his eyes alight with anticipation. What pleasure! How he enjoys building his house—or is it a bridge? No matter.

And then—he lifts his foot and kicks. The blocks tumble down. No more house, or bridge. One moment of anger, and wham!

His pleasure is destroyed, and the child cries, bitterly, wondering what he has done—and why.

As an adult, you must learn to rise above the child-like state. You must learn to prepare each day for a day of pleasure, and you must learn to defeat your propensities for self-destruction. And, the more positive your focus, the greater will be your delight in yourself.

10. Truth-seeking

You seek the truth about yourself, and the truth should enable you to increase your self-acceptance.

Not that the truth about you is necessarily

that you are absolutely wonderful without quali-
fication. Not at all. For you are a human being.

When you seek the truth about yourself, you
should acknowledge that you are a complex composite of many forces. You should acknowledge
that you have your ups and downs, your highs and
lows, your storms and stresses. You must also
know that you are a person who is thoughtful and
thoughtless, tormented and tranquil, tough and
timid. You are a series of contradictions, and yet
you make sense.

One goal all human beings share, and that is
the desire to live. By living I do not mean vege-
tative existence, I mean happiness.

Our stay in this world is a short one. Death,
unfortunately, comes to us all. You know that; I
know that. We have all known the death of loved
ones, as well as the death of people with whom
our acquaintance was more casual. We cannot
deny the existence of death; to deny it is an irre-
sponsible evasion.

What we must do, in our truth-seeking which
includes our acknowledgment of the reality of
death, is to live fully—while the gift of life is our
privilege.

11. Active awareness

Self-acceptance means a continuing sense of
active awareness of your identity as a human
being.

You must be aware of the sheer joy in giving
—which is often much greater than that in taking.

One Sunday morning not too long ago I arrived in San Francisco from Sacramento. A man
in chauffeur's uniform who owned his own lim-
ousine drove me to my hotel where I would rest up
before delivering a lecture. He said to me, "I have

a number of people who are customers and I'm there whenever they call—even if it's 4 A.M., anytime. It makes me feel good. I feel I'm needed."

You must give; you must feel needed; you must feel an active awareness of yourself as a giver in life.

Active awareness means that you adapt yourself to a changing world. Each day is different and as you adapt yourself to changing conditions your image of yourself changes. You accept yourself in your complexity, and in your awareness of the complexity and diversity of human life.

12. Nucleus of affirmation

You must affirm and reaffirm your belief in yourself. This belief must be rocklike.

You look at a calendar, and you see days and dates. Do you believe they are accurate?

You do. It is from a reputable source, it is a legitimate calendar, and of course you know the dates are accurate. You believe, and your belief is well founded.

So must you affirm and reaffirm your belief in yourself. No material possessions are more important; no amount of money is more important.

13. Concentration plus

Concentration can be plus or minus. If you have a goal, your concentration is purposeful. If you have no goal, you cannot concentrate creatively. With concentration plus you increase your sense of self-acceptance.

Avoid the dread disease of your times—*self-imagitis*.

And what is self-imagitis? It is wounded self-image. The person with the wounded self-image may have no high temperature and his life may not be in danger, but he certainly needs help—

just as a person with pneumonia needs help. There is no physical infection, but the pain is real.

The alcoholic drinks in his search for oblivion or for relief from his heartaches.

The person with self-imagitis inflicts wounds upon his opinion of himself. He tortures himself. He hates himself.

Cure self-imagitis with concentration plus—concentration plus on worthwhile goals. Bolster your sense of self-esteem, and march on your goals.

14. Enthusiastic effort

Self-acceptance is not passive. It takes hard work; it takes enthusiastic effort.

It may be easier to lapse into self-defeating apathy. It may be easier to tell yourself that life is rough and that you are a born loser. It may be easier to tell yourself that you're no good, and that you never were any good. These negating ways of thinking may come easier than true self-acceptance.

If you feel enthusiasm for painting your house or mowing your lawn, or mopping the kitchen floor or washing your car, surely you can feel enthusiasm for that greatest of all tasks—the development of your capacity for self-acceptance.

YOUR LIBERATION

We human beings, outside penitentiary walls yet so often emotionally imprisoned, we must learn to liberate ourselves.

We must stop locking up our personalities.

We must stop imprisoning our emotions.

We must stop guarding our feelings so carefully that we have lost the capacity for joy.

Sometimes, walking in the street, you may see an armored truck lumber by, loaded with money and guarded with enormous vigilance.

This vigilance is of course necessary.

But you, must you lock up your feelings? Must you imprison your personality?

By and large the answer is no. At times you must, in demanding circumstances, but as a rule, no.

Then how do you liberate yourself? How do you find fulfillment?

Through self-acceptance.

Through accepting yourself in our uncertain world, through accepting yourself in our troubled world, through accepting yourself in our world which seems to pose so many problems for people.

7

WINNING THE BATTLE WITH YOUR CONSCIENCE

You have read the first six chapters and have digested my ideas on gaining self-fulfillment.

"Very good," you say to yourself. "These ideas will help me."

"But," you add, "my conscience won't let me reach self-fulfillment."

A very important *but*, indeed. And one that you must learn to overcome.

For down through history "conscience" has tortured people, eating into their minds to destroy them from within, transforming winners into losers, happy people into suffering wretches.

And down through history it is "conscience" that has made cowards of the brave. Poets and philosophers have filled many pages of anthologies with descriptions of the evil effects of conscience upon mere human beings unfitted to wrestle with such a scourge.

My view is a little different. I see conscience more as a battle, a battle that you must win—a battle between our success mechanism and our failure mechanism. Win this battle and you are on your way to self-fulfillment; lose it and, overcome by negative feelings, you may tell yourself that "your conscience bothers you."

In World War II, during the Battle of the Bulge, American soldiers fought off fierce German counterattacks and then went forward again. Finally, the coordinated efforts of all our soldiers and those of our allies won the war.

And you too must do battle; your success instincts must engage and defeat your failure instincts.

When you win this crucial battle, then you will forget all about your conscience.

VICTORY OVER YOUR CONSCIENCE

Now for our battle plan. Let us spell it out.

1. **C** Confrontation.
2. **O** Opportunity versus Oppression.
3. **N** Negative Feelings versus Positive Feelings.
4. **S** Search for Self-Respect or Failure.
5. **C** Cooperation or Non-Cooperation with Your Self-Image.
6. **I** Imagination Plus versus Imagination Minus.
7. **E** Enterprise Plus versus Enterprise Minus.
8. **N** Nucleus of Faith or Despair.
9. **C** Courage to Win.
10. **E** Empathy.

This is our battle plan. Now let us see if we can execute it properly.

1. Confrontation

Conscience implies a confrontation between two—a conflict and an attempt at readjustment that often is not successful. This confrontation is, in its essence, a meeting of two forces who are unable to see the same thing the same way and who, opinionated, harden their opposing points of view.

Thus we often find that there is little likelihood of compromise or of change, and a status quo takes root that becomes most difficult to budge; yet this divergency of viewpoint is essential.

Now, more specifically, to what confrontation do we refer? To the one between you and the negative forces within you.

This may be a difficult confrontation; yet you must attempt it, and you must win out.

When two nations are at war, or when they oppose each other in the United Nations so implacably that there is no real communication, they are not on speaking terms with each other and much misunderstanding is often the result. Both are reluctant to change, hostile, ready to retaliate quickly—like two people who are married who have lost interest in each other; no love remains, but they hold onto each other in a communication of dubious value.

All right, but what about your confrontation? What about your cold war?

You must make it a strong fight; you must gear your positive forces into a compressed formation, and sweep down powerfully to overwhelm the negative forces inside you.

You must stop downgrading yourself.

You must stop worrying about every little thing that might happen.

You must stop hating yourself for every little fault.

2. Opportunity versus oppression

Within us is an eternal conflict; between your

seizing opportunity and your avoidance of your opportunity.

We all have goals, but many of us are afraid to reach out to them. Perhaps we rationalize, telling ourselves that when opportunity knocks we will be ready for it.

But opportunity does not usually knock. *You* must create opportunity. You must create it with rational, clear thinking which you project out into strong performance. You must take the initiative.

Too many of us move toward oppression, not opportunity.

In the course of this painful conflict, you may use your conscience to inflict defeat on yourself.

"I cannot seize this opportunity, I cannot reach my goal," you may tell yourself. "It's because of my conscience. My conscience would bother me."

Or you may say to yourself, "Someday I'll tackle this goal, but not today. If I tackled it today, my conscience would bother me."

Nonsense. Stop using your conscience as an excuse for reinforcing your failure mechanism. Choose opportunity, reject oppression.

Let me, however, make one qualifying remark: In advising you to do battle with the conscience that cripples you, I am *not* counseling you to go against your good, sound ethical ideas or to throw away your reasonable notions of what constitutes right or wrong. I am *not* counseling you to go around stepping on people's toes or pushing their faces in to get to your goals. I *am* counseling you to move forward toward your goals in a positive spirit, not trying to hurt others, *and* not using rationalizations and evasions in the name of conscience to defeat yourself.

Because the individual with a burdensome

conscience can allow himself no pleasure, no opportunity, no goal-striving.

To him they are all criminal, and he imprisons all his good feelings in submerging himself in that oppressive guilt.

Like a girl who came to see me a few years ago. She was nineteen, an age of hope and yearning for good things in the present and future, but she lived with constant guilt and constant self-hatred. With her conscience crushing her sense of self-esteem, she needed drugs to give her a lift. She took LSD on and off for two years; it didn't work—not really. While on a "trip," she recalled, she felt she was "falling in space . . . falling . . . falling—like a shooting star," but then she was back in the world of reality and of living with her conscience and it was a world of guilt that she inhabited.

I looked at her. She was twenty pounds overweight; her face was sad, as if she carried the burden of the world's troubles on her shoulders.

"Do you live with your parents?" I asked her.

"No. I ran away from home when I was sixteen."

"Do you get along all right with your mother?"

"I love her," she said, and started to cry. Once she had started, she could not stop. She cried and cried. "I'm sorry," she said finally, wiping her eyes.

"For what? For crying? For showing how you feel? What's wrong with crying?"

"I love her," she said.

"Your mother? That's fine. It's a wonderful feeling to love your mother."

She was crying again. "But it's all my fault," she wailed through the tears. "It's all my fault."

"What's your fault?"

"I can never forgive myself. It was my fault. I can never forgive myself."

"For what? Tell me what happened."

She was crying again. "How can I tell you? You'll think I'm terrible."

"No, I won't. Tell me about it."

She looked at me uncertainly. "I was thirteen," she said, wavering, her eyes searching my face for confirmation of her conscience's judgment of Guilty, "and I wanted some clothes for camp. We lived outside of town and my mother didn't feel like driving in to buy them. I pestered her; I had to have the clothes, I told her. She said no, she was tired, but I kept after her, pestering her —until she drove the car into town."

"What then?"

She looked at me blankly; a mask seemed to blanket her face, removing all feelings, paralyzing her. "She did what I asked. She drove into town. Another car crashed into our car and my mother was hurt. She has been a cripple ever since." Inert, lifeless, a rag doll. Then, suddenly, the feelings fought through, and she was crying, a deluge of tears.

"I'm glad you can cry," I said.

"Yes," she wailed. "I deserve to cry—for what I did to my mother."

"That's not what I mean. I mean that it's good for you to get your feelings out like that; it cleanses you."

"I'll cry all my life," she said.

"But it wasn't your fault," I said.

She didn't hear me. "She's in a wheelchair."

"I know how you feel, but it was not your fault. You did not drive the car that crashed into yours, you did not cripple her."

"If only I hadn't pestered her."

"You still love your mother?"

118

"Yes."

"Do you want to make her feel better—even if she is crippled?"

"Of course."

"Then, forgive yourself," I said. "You are so miserable that you make your parents miserable. Since you were thirteen, you've given up on yourself. How about giving yourself a chance to live again—now, in the present? If you feel happier, you'll make them happier. Your father, too. Does your father love you?"

"They both do."

"Then try to get the better of your nagging conscience, and make them happy as you make yourself happy. Forgive yourself. Your conscience is oppressing you; it is tyrannizing over you. Because of this, you do not see your opportunities for full living. Win out over your conscience; forgive yourself."

"I'll try," she said.

I asked if there was any work she wanted to do. She said she would like to teach elocution, help kids to express themselves, and I encouraged her to move toward her goal.

A few years later, I was giving a seminar to sales executives in Palm Springs, California, and just before getting up on the podium to lecture, I saw a man in his early fifties rushing toward me. He grabbed my hand and shook it vigorously. He told me about his daughter, how I had helped her, how she was now teaching elocution, how she was beginning to find a sense of fulfillment.

3. Negative feelings versus positive feelings

Within us all is the conflict between disbelief and belief, between love and hate, between joy and misery, between the will for survival and the will for destruction. We are fragile, easily hurt. Ardently we wish to be perfect; when we make a mistake, we may feel ashamed of it. Many of us carry with us feelings of inferiority and may try to protect ourselves from the outside world by assuming a false armor of superiority which is all too vulnerable. We walk away from reality, from the world, even from ourselves into a dark, troubled tunnel in our minds, crying out to all who would listen that the world is cruel, that Fate is against us, that other people are without heart or conscience.

Yes, too often we succumb to negative feelings, and too often we crush our positive feelings under the weight of negation.

Now conscience can have an uplifting meaning. Some people act on conscience in a positive and deeply ethical sense, trying to do good—for themselves and for others.

Too often, however, people use conscience in an unrealistically prohibitive sense, reinforcing negative feelings and driving them toward frustration and away from self-fulfillment.

Do not let your conscience make unreasonable demands of you! Make your conscience be reasonable! Do not let a tyrannical conscience crush your positive feelings! You deserve better.

4. Search for self-respect or failure

This is the usual conflict between your success and your failure instincts.

The conflict between sense of direction or goal and no direction or frustration.

The conflict between understanding leading to respectful relations between people and misunderstanding leading to failures in communication between people.

The conflict between self-acceptance leading upward and self-denial leading downward.

The conflict between fulfillment and emptiness.

Between esteem and disesteem.

Between love and resentment.

Always we are searching for one or for the other.

For we are complex people; we have two sides—or more—to us. We are Siamese twins locked together and, in a sense, maturity means we have gained the capacity to be our own plastic surgeon and skillfully separate these twins. We are capable of self-respect and of failure; we are on a seesaw rotating back and forth and it is up to us to give the greater weight to self-respect and to conditions in our lives that will gain for us increased self-respect.

You must have a real confrontation with your conscience; you must use your conscience as your ally, not as your enemy. In your search for self-respect, win out by first winning your battle with your conscience and making it a friend.

How?

Let me tell you a story:

It's about a woman I shall call Mrs. Molly A., a small woman in her early sixties, a widow, whose conscience told her that in her station in life and at her age it was proper for her to stay at home and read a book or knit something. She should not—according to her conscience, reinforced by the opinions of her daughter—walk around everywhere in the outside world, talking to people and looking about her at all the curious features of life.

Then she met a man who talked to her in a companionable way and, trying to lift her spirits, suggested that she buy a new hat.

She hadn't done this for a long time—the idea almost frightened her: but she went ahead toward her goal. That is she went to a hat shop.

In the hat shop, however, she got discouraged. When she tried a hat on and looked in the mirror, the hat and her face simply did not go together. Her face, she decided sadly, was too old for the hat.

But back home an idea came to her; the idea took hold of her and frightened her. *No,* her conscience started to tell her, *this idea was impossible.*

But once again she silenced a conscience that really was unreasonable and asked herself, why not? Why not get her face lifted?

She examined her face in the bathroom mirror of her apartment. Sagging cheeks, and heavy folds of wrinkles around her eyes. Perhaps a plastic surgeon could help her. She would check it out.

And so, overcoming the prohibitions of her conscience, Mrs. Molly A. came to visit me in my office and we became good buddies. After the operation her face had a new-found beauty.

With her ability to direct herself toward such a well-motivated goal, Mrs. Molly A. felt a new sense of self-satisfaction and even seemed to be considering the also new idea of marriage with the man who had inspired her.

This is an interesting story because it shows how a person can insist on goals and esteem and fulfillment and overcome the tyranny of conscience.

5. Cooperation or non-cooperation with your self-image

You may or may not be an architect, but you have a blueprint of the person you believe you are or which you want to be. Still, how do you work with this blueprint? What do you do with it?

Do you cooperate with your self-image? Or do you refuse to cooperate with it? Do you even disrupt it?

As I have elaborated in a number of my books, your self-image is your guiding star. It is your self-image which, in large measure, drives you on to success or drags you down to failure. It is your self-image—your concept of yourself, your feeling about your worth—that determines in large measure your feeling toward other people and their feeling toward you. No goal is more worthwhile than building up this image of yourself; no more inspiring goal do I know than strengthening this conception of yourself.

But, to repeat, do you cooperate with your self-image—or is your policy one of non-cooperation?

You should ask yourself this question every day when you wake up. And then you should make it your goal for that day—and for every day—to cooperate with your self-image.

What does this have to do with conscience?

Well, in a way your self-image is your conscience. When your self-image is strong and you feel happy and successful, does your conscience nag you? Or does your conscience bother you generally when your self-image is weak and you feel revulsion toward yourself?

So every day work to cooperate with your self-image and you will find you are winning your battle over your self-defeating conscience.

6. Imagination plus versus imagination minus

How sharp is this distinction—between imagination plus and imagination minus?

Imagination plus. You think creatively, you plot your goals, you envision bright prospects and ways to make these prospects reality. You see in your mind ways to improve your life and the lives of those whom you love. Your direction is forward and your feeling is constructive. You value your great power of imagination, understanding it is a great gift which God has bestowed on you.

Imagination minus. When you see yourself in your mind, you cannot stand the sight of yourself. You misuse "conscience" repeatedly to block yourself from your goals: your "conscience" bothers you any time you might achieve a success or feel happy or see a bright picture of the future. Thus you feel apprehensive, your mind buzzes with anxieties, and you obsess yourself with your past mistakes and failures.

Do yourself a favor, and make it a daily goal to work toward imagination plus. Make your self-image a productive image and envision inspiring, realistic goals—no matter how small these goals may be. Concentrate on the great goal that is common to all mankind: the desire to live and to be happy.

Then go after it your own way.

7. Enterprise plus versus enterprise minus

Here we carry imagination into action—into enterprise.

But what kind of enterprise? Enterprise plus? Or enterprise minus?

Enterprise plus. How you value your time! You use it so well. You make every minute of the day count; you do not "pass the time" or "kill time." You are aware of the great value of time, and you give it to the goals that are meaningful to you, to people who are meaningful to you. You take action to help yourself, and you are also enterprising when it comes to helping your human brothers and sisters. You cram your days full of good deeds. You put your full weight into everything you do.

Enterprise minus. Your life is an exercise in passivity and nothingness and you continually find excuses for keeping it this way. For one thing your conscience seems to bother you all the time —or much of the time. Your conscience rules you; no matter what you do you feel guilty, so naturally you do nothing.

If you are an enterprise-minus person, you must learn to change. People do change sometimes. Even at the age of sixty-eight. Like a man I'll call Mr. H.

At sixty-eight, Mr. H. was a strictly enterprise-minus individual. His daily routine was rigidly set and absolutely monotonous. Up early in the morning, light breakfast, morning newspaper and cigar purchases, then to his favorite park bench to read his paper and smoke his cigar.

Lunch at noon for Mr. H., then back to his hotel room for a nap. Later on in the afternoon, back to the park for some more time on the bench, then back to the hotel to freshen up, then dinner. His evening followed a similar boring, regulated pattern.

On his sixty-eighth birthday, Mr. H. celebrated by following his usual routine: from the usual breakfast to the usual newspaper and cigar to the usual park bench.

But there was one change, and this change skyrocketed Mr. H. from the world of the enterprise-minus to the world of the enterprise-plus.

Mr. H. became the owner of a puppy.

It was all sheer accident. He met a down-and-out looking man on a street corner, gave him a dollar out of sympathy, and found that the man, running away, had left him with a puppy.

What could he do? Mr. H. looked at the puppy, and the puppy looked at him. The little dog looked hungry; Mr. H. took him to his favorite lunchroom and bought him hamburger. The puppy wolfed it down as if he hadn't eaten for days; probably he hadn't.

Truly it was an absurd puppy—its ancestry seemed to be dachshund, sheep dog, airedale, and bulldog. A funny-looking dog indeed, but he attached himself warmly to Mr. H. And so Mr. H. was, to his surprise, a dog owner.

He named the dog after the middle name of his favorite American author—Fenimore.

And, with the acquisition of Fenimore, change after change came into Mr. H.'s life.

First, he moved from his hotel—pets were not allowed—and ventured forth into a double room with kitchenette in a rooming house.

Then, he found himself talking to people in the streets, people who were attracted by Fenimore's peculiar charms. People could not help laughing at Fenimore, who was such a friendly, funny-looking little dog.

A group of young boys had a baseball team, and they asked Mr. H. if the little dog could be their mascot. Of course the pup would have to come to every baseball game—and their schedule called for a game every day for the next month, and perhaps all summer.

Mr. H. thought it over. He would miss the dog's company; he was beginning to like him. But then a new idea came to him: he would attend the games with his dog.

And so, at sixty-eight, Mr. H. found himself

on the move—an enterprising young man in his retirement years, growing younger every day.

The changes grew ever more surprising. Fenimore, as mascot, was active, and Mr. H. felt he wanted to be active, too. He began umpiring the boys' baseball games. He was an expert umpire.

And then came love. He had been married; his wife had died three years earlier, and he never expected to remarry, it seems safe to assume. But now he was courting a widow, a very charming woman in her early sixties, a small woman whom he advised to buy a hat to cheer her up but who had been discouraged by the sight of her sagging, wrinkled face in a mirror. Winning a victory over negative forces in herself, this woman was enthusiastic over the improvements made in her appearance.

That's right. Mr. H. was now seeing Mrs. Molly A., about whom I've just written, and the question was now: Was marriage in the air?

Quite a story—and an amazing change from enterprise minus to enterprise plus.

What is my point? Certainly *not* that you should rush right out and buy yourself a dog—even though the little dog did Mr. H. a world of good.

My point is this: Change is always possible, even at sixty-eight, and you should always strive to improve yourself, to become more enterprising, to reach out toward enterprise plus.

Your conscience may hold you back; don't let it: You may remind yourself that you're a rather worthless person, really, that you have spent your life making mistakes for which you deserve punishment: and that punishment is to have to endure more years suffering under the tyranny of your ruthless conscience.

Don't do this to yourself! Give yourself life, hope, and exciting enterprises.

8. Nucleus of faith or despair

Faith is a goal in the making; despair is a goal you have forsaken. Faith is movement toward self-fulfillment; despair is movement away from your goals to frustration. Faith is the flowing, kinetic pulse of life; despair is the passive, apathetic retreat from life.

In your person you must consolidate the qualities that are you. You must choose to develop a nucleus of faith in yourself, and to turn your back on the attitude that brings you inner death —despair.

Conscience can play a role in this important choice. If your self-image is weak and you persist in disliking and undermining yourself, prohibitions from your conscience will run roughshod over your positive drives and you will allow yourself neither peace of mind nor the refreshment of opportunity, neither the pursuit of goals nor the attainment of pleasure.

Give your conscience a positive role. Build faith in yourself and give credit to your conscience. Let your good conscience guide you—without fear—in establishing a nucleus of faith in yourself. Let your tolerant conscience give you support in times of stress so that you can have faith in your ability to survive stress.

9. Courage to win

We have already discussed the question of confrontation and the battle between the negative and positive forces inside all of us. To win this battle, it almost goes without saying that you need courage.

Courage on the battlefield is obvious and everyone knows about this form of courage.

Everyone knows about the infantryman charging forward—through bullets, through mine fields, through artillery shells—toward his objective.

Everyone knows about the medical aid man risking his life carrying wounded men back to safer areas where they may receive treatment.

Everyone knows about the airplane pilot guiding his craft through heavily defended sky to key areas where his mates can drop bombs and cripple the enemy.

Everyone knows about this kind of winning courage.

But what about that silent, little seen form of courage that means fulfillment or frustration?

What about the courage to win out over a tyrannizing conscience that says to you: *You're no good because you're not perfect?*

What about courage to win out over a critical conscience that says to you: *You should feel guilty because of what you did a few years ago?*

What about the courage to win out over an inhuman conscience that says to you: *You are unworthy because every day you make a mistake?*

To me there is no greater courage than this —the courage to win out over your own negation.

10. Empathy

Getting along with your conscience involves an empathy with all sides of yourself. In a way this is a play on words since the word *empathy* is generally used to indicate a fellow feeling for somebody else. Still, you have many sides—in this sense, you are almost somebody else—and so I will take some liberties and use this word in this connection.

In developing a fellow feeling for yourself, you adopt a humble attitude toward your shortcomings—but you do not reject yourself for them.

And, biggest weapon against a stern and cruel conscience, you forgive yourself.

You forgive yourself for your errors of commission and omission.

You forgive yourself for the past, the present, and the future.

Your forgiveness is complete. You don't have to pretend you're someone else because you accept yourself as you are.

This is real fellow feeling toward yourself; this is the way to live with your conscience.

This is the way to be a friend to yourself.

A BLUEPRINT FOR BETTER LIVING

And so we have spelled out a blueprint for better living.

Because in combating the disastrous effects of a stern and unjust conscience—and in winning the battle against such a punishing conscience—a person can attain for himself new frontiers in the great exploratory search for inner peace of mind.

And this—more than any house, more than any automobile, more than any stock on the stock market—will lead you to a quality of self-fulfillment that is increasingly uncommon in a world which seems to have forgotten many of the answers to questions of human happiness.

Don't let your conscience rule you; you rule your conscience.

Every day work to build up your self-image. Every day work to reactivate the functioning of your success mechanism. Every day feel a new compassion for yourself, and a new sense of self-respect.

Then, as time passes, you will feel a new

confidence—and you will no longer fear your conscience.

This is a major step toward better living. It is a major step toward achieving self-fulfillment.

8

FROM LONELINESS TO HAPPINESS

In this chapter we will pave a new road, leading, hopefully, from loneliness to happiness. This is a wonderful road indeed. On this new highway there are no speed limits at all—and more power to you!

We will concentrate on loneliness because we are interested in achieving self-fulfillment, and loneliness and self-fulfillment cannot comfortably coexist. Indeed, they are contradictions in that self-fulfillment implies a peaceful resolution of one's aspirations and realities and an integration of one's personality; while loneliness implies a separation from the positive side of oneself and from others in our world.

I see loneliness as a component of the failure mechanism within us; it is a manifestation of unbelief in ourselves which causes us to withdraw from the positive side of ourselves. We will analyze these forces of unbelief so that, seeing your enemy, you will be able to combat negative forces. Then we will analyze the opposite factors in yourself —those that make up your success instincts and that constitute your success mechanism—so that you can move away from loneliness onto the road to happiness in the world of people.

Many symptoms of unbelief operate to produce loneliness so I can give you only a fragmentary list. How many of these symptoms do you recognize in yourself?

U: Unconvinced that you can reach happiness.

Uncertain, about past, present, and future.

Unacceptable—to yourself.

Unprepared for the better you.

Unfair to your sense of self-respect.

Unwilling to reach out toward fulfillment.

Unready for a creative day.

N: No basic faith in yourself.

No sense of self-fulfillment.

No resiliency when you fail.

No goals.

No-no, instead of yes-yes.

B: Being basically untrue to yourself.

Being fearful and insecure.

Being a chronic complainer.

Being what you're not.

E: Entertaining negating feelings.

Engaged in continual resentment.

Evil—to yourself.

Envious of others.

L: Looking backward, in rage, not forward in hope.

Living with boredom.

Leaving your resources unused.

Lethargy as a way of life.

I: Ineffectual as a personality.

Intolerant—of yourself and others.

Incarcerated in a dungeon you have created.

Incapacitated in despair.

E: Evading your sense of integrity.

Eliminating your sense of worth.
Entertaining failure.

F: Forgetful of your real capacities.
Famine of mind, famine of spirit.
Failure to forgive—yourself and
others.
False to your true self.

Now how many of these symptoms of unbelief do you see in yourself? Be honest about it; evasion will only injure you. Don't expect yourself to be so perfect! The more honest you are in evaluating your own symptoms of unbelief, the more possible it will be for you to replace them with symptoms of your own affirmative qualities.

And at this point, aware of the connection between the failure mechanism and unbelief and loneliness, suppose that we study the other faces of loneliness so that we can change this face. As a plastic surgeon, I have spent my life improving the faces of people; just as important—perhaps even more so—is the need to change the face of loneliness, of failure, to a face of health and success and happiness.

THE TEN FACES OF LONELINESS

Once again, let us spell out for you. This time, LONELINESS.

1. **L** Limitation (over-limitation).
2. **O** Obstinacy.
3. **N** Neglect of Self-respect.
4. **E** Eviction of Sense of Self.
5. **L** Lamentation.
6. **I** Impotent Emptiness.

7. **N** Nostalgia for the Past.
8. **E** Elimination.
9. **S** Selfishness.
10. **S** Separation.

We will now analyze these ten faces of loneliness and this time we will also spell out the reverse face: the face of happiness.

1. Limitation (over-limitation)

There is limitation in all of us as a natural consequence of our living in a civilized state, for civilization implies guiding, restricting rules whereby we can all live together in harmony.

But over-limitation is something else. This implies an unnecessary, fearful constriction of the personality which is characteristic of loneliness. There is nothing wrong with a self-limitation which safeguards us from extending ourselves beyond our capacities, but a self-limitation which goes beyond this can amount to an imprisonment of our basic personality that is one of the tragedies of modern life.

The reverse of LIMITATION is LIBERTY.

Leave yesterday behind and look for goals that will free your creative capacities.

Inaugurate a start toward better living and involve yourself with others.

Be yourself as much as you can. Be less critical of yourself so you can live a little.

Evade negation. Help yourself live more today by bringing back the confidence of past successes.

Relax. Renew yourself every day; you redeem yourself when you refuse to live with resentment.

Try to reach your goals every day. Break

out of your self-imposed jail and move toward them.

Yearn for improvement all the time. Free your capacities for forgiveness, and then go!

2. Obstinacy

Unfortunately, we see obstinacy almost every day of our lives. We turn on our television sets and we see it: in negotiations that seem interminable, in fixed positions that seldom change, in disputes that seem to know no end, in human frictions that produce despair.

And, of course, we see it in people we know. Many of us are obstinate; we are opinionated; we cling to our fixed positions and insist on forcing our opinions on others.

This fixedness of outlook may intensify our feelings of estrangement from other sides of ourselves; it may also evoke antagonism in others. We may thus find that obstinacy brings on, and intensifies, loneliness.

The reverse of OBSTINACY is OPPORTUNITY.

Obliterate the scars of negative feelings.

Practice self-acceptance.

Prepare for creativity every day.

Obey the good rules as you play fair with yourself and then with others.

Respect yourself first, then others.

To be better or not to be better; it is this question that, with apologies to William Shakespeare, you must answer.

Understand your own needs first, and then the needs of others.

Nourish the conviction that you have the capacity to rise above your mistakes.

Imagine that you can achieve a goal that is realistic for you, then move toward it.

Turn toward people with friendliness.
You belong to yourself; you can trust yourself.

3. Neglect of self-respect

When you fail yourself, in that you cannot find it within yourself to give yourself the sense of self-respect that you need, you are guilty of a terrible crime toward yourself. Stop neglecting yourself; when you do this to yourself, you are building a foundation of loneliness difficult to overcome.

Do you neglect to lock your home when you go to sleep at night? Do you neglect to pay your taxes when they are due? Do you neglect to visit your dentist when a tooth causes you great pain?

Probably not. But, then, why neglect to give yourself the sense of self-respect that feeds your soul and that gives stature to your humanity?

Let me tell you another story. I love to tell stories, and this one is pertinent.

A man told me this story in St. Clair, near Chicago, about a young woman who had listened to my lecture in Cincinnati which I delivered to some insurance people.

First, some background:

After my lecture this girl—beautiful and in her twenties, I would say—walked over to speak to me. She asked me how she could overcome her terrible feeling of loneliness. "I loved someone and married him," she wept. "But he divorced me."

I asked her why he had left her, but she said she didn't know, that she had done the best she knew how to make him happy.

"You must understand that you must not hold yourself responsible for what he has done," I said. "You can't control his actions. How are you responsible?"

"I don't know, but still I feel very sad and lonely. I guess I love him, still."

"I can see that," I said. "But listen to me: you are young and I've lived long enough to give you some fatherly advice—on the basis of the heartaches I have endured in my life. You cannot hold yourself accountable for the actions of other people. You must accept responsibility for yourself and live today. Set constructive goals to help yourself today. Build your good opinion of yourself; see in your mind your good moments, use your imagination to see again the side of yourself that you like."

Anyway, she said thanks and about a half year later I met this man in St. Clair. On the earlier occasion he had listened to me, too, as I tried to help the anxious, lonely woman.

"I've got news for you," he said to me. "Remember that girl who cried that other time I met you?"

"Yes."

"Well, she married again."

"Fine."

"Not only that, but she remarried the same guy."

I expressed surprise and asked what had happened.

"He phoned Cincinnati to say hello—he was living in California. But she acted different. She didn't plead with him to come back; she just acted friendly and let it go at that. She had built up her self-image. She had won a new sense of self-respect. She respected herself too much to act like a beggar.

"She sounded like a different person to him —like the woman he had always longed for—and so he flew to Cincinnati and found there a woman with self-respect. So he remarried her."

And this story has a moral: that self-respect is our goal, that we must not neglect it.

The reverse of NEGLECT is UNDERSTANDING.

Utilize your past successes today.

Never neglect your human dignity.

Devote some time each day to your improvement as a human being.

Enthusiasm for your goals; develop this quality, vital for your self-fulfillment.

Resolve each day to make yourself a better person.

Select goals that are realistic for you.

Take time off every day to build a better you.

Achieve a measure of fulfillment every day.

No task is impossible if you understand your limits.

Decide to be yourself, not an imitation of someone else.

Infuse yourself with optimism.

Nourish your real potential.

Give to others; you'll feel good when you do.

4. Eviction of sense of self

This is a dread eviction; it is worse than the most horrible eviction from one's home. And no landlord does it to you; you do it to yourself.

Eviction of sense of self and loneliness are almost synonymous, for when you lose this comforting feeling of your identity, you are lonely indeed. No material well-being can console you for such a loss.

The world of loneliness is barren and desolate. It is unfruitful and unproductive. You do not want to live in such a world; you do not want to evict your sense of self.

Instead, how about CONVICTION?

Concentrate on strengthening your self-image.

Overcome your feeling of isolation from others.

Never walk away from yourself; support yourself when things get tough.

Veer toward your past successes.

Invite success, not failure.

Consent to let the past stay in the past; bury your grudges.

Try to upgrade your sense of self.

Instruct yourself in self-acceptance.

Offer yourself your friendship.

Never give up your sense of self.

5. Lamentation

Lamentation as a way of life leads to loneliness. Inevitably the individual who drowns himself and others in misery feels alone—alienated from himself and from others.

We all know grief in our lives. We all know heartache, and trouble, and problems, and misfortune. Under the weight of life's woes, all of us at times feel mournful and the need for lamentation. And certainly there is nothing wrong with this.

But lamentation as a way of life is something else. For grief must somewhere, somehow, know an end. A human being can stand just so much unhappiness, just so much lamentation over his grievances. Then he must find a way to live with himself, or else surrender to an unbearable wave of loneliness that will seep over the shoreline of his existence and proceed to sweep away the good cement of his constructive foundations.

A friend of mine showed me a letter; it was

from her son, who was in Vietnam. She was terrified something would happen to him. She worried about it during the days and slept little worrying about it nights. Of course, there was a very realistic basis for her fear; still, what good did all her lamentation and suffering do her? And, further, how could it help her son, all this lamentation?

She had been an overpossessive mother, she admitted, and had treated him as if he were a child all his life. And, in her son's letter, I read one sentence that lingered in my mind: "Mother, don't kill yourself before you're dead."

You, too, don't kill yourself before you're dead. Don't kill yourself with endless lamentation; don't kill yourself with endless grief. Learn to live creatively.

I have known grief; I have known lamentation. I have lived through them, and then gone on to better days. And this, too, you must do.

The reverse of LAMENTATION is INVOLVEMENT.

Insist on your right to be a constructive member of the human family.

No one can force you into isolation.

Vanquish the fear that grief can make you helpless.

Obliterate the failures of the past.

Live now—in times of stress, in times of grief, in times of heartbreak.

Volunteer to move toward a new and inspiring goal.

Exercise your ability to share with others.

Make certain you move toward the world.

Engage in constructive pursuits.

Never neglect your friendship for others.

Today is another day for you to reach out for heartwarming involvements with others.

6. Impotent emptiness

When you feel this way, you are barely half-alive. You have surrendered much of your life urge, you have given up much of the precious gift that God has bestowed upon you. In this half-living state naturally you succumb to loneliness and to negation.

The impotently empty individual withdraws from life, fearing to test his powers in a world of change and danger. In fear, he prefers loneliness to the trauma of challenge and uncertainty. Fear rules his life. He is passive to the tyranny of this negative emotion and does not have enough faith in possibilities to take a chance and propel himself out into the world of action and adventure.

In a sense, he is ignorant. Fearing to know himself, separated from his creative powers, he remains ignorant of the rich emotional resources he may bury inside himself.

Let me tell you another story:

It is about a middle-aged woman who felt impotent and empty. A schoolteacher, functional, married many years, with three children, but in her feelings—empty and despairing.

She had lost her father when she was six. She had loved him and longed for his love when he died. She remembered him sitting by the window looking for her when she was six, before he died. He had held her hand—proud of her—the first time he had taken her to school. And, then, a heart attack, and he was gone.

I talked to her about this tragedy; what a tragedy for a girl of six to lose her beloved father!

"You feel he rejected you by dying, by leaving you?"

"Yes, doctor."

"And your mother?"

"She died thirty-three years later. We loved each other."

"When your mother died, did you feel that she too rejected you?"

"Yes."

"You didn't want her to leave you?"

"No. When she died, I felt so empty and so lonely and powerless. I wished I were dead, too."

"And what about your marriage?" (We had talked about this previously: I knew quite a bit about her background.)

She talked about her twenty-seven years of marriage: her three children, how she loved her husband, how he did not return her love, how now her children were grown up and married and her husband was, she knew, having an affair with a younger woman. He had wanted to leave her two years before, but he still lived with her.

"If he walked out on me, I would just as soon die," she cried out. "I feel so empty. I've been thinking of suicide."

"No matter what," I said, "you must respect yourself. If he leaves you, if he stays, you must look at yourself with kind eyes and give yourself respect."

"But I can't live without him."

"Yes, you can live without him—if you hold onto your dignity and accept yourself, if you keep working to fulfill yourself as a human being." I understood, of course, that there was doubtless some relation in her mind between her parents leaving her through death and the threat of her husband leaving her.

Still despairing, she left me, but when I saw her a year later she felt more hope. Her efforts to build her own self-esteem had paid off. Her husband had fought with the other woman and broken up with her. Her relations with her husband still were far from perfect, but he was becoming more attentive and she hoped for further improvement.

She felt less impotent emptiness, more creative urge toward growth and fulfillment. Imperfect, inconclusive, but she was moving in the right direction.

The opposite of IMPOTENT EMPTINESS is ENTHUSIASM.

Engage yourself spiritedly in creative pursuits.

Never lose your sense of the wonder in life.

Try every day to overcome your boredom through worthwhile goals.

Have faith in your powers.

Understand that life can be fun.

Select goals that are realistic for you, then move out to reach them.

Investigate your real worth so that you can feel good about yourself.

Accept your shortcomings so that you can feel good even when you fail.

See yourself at your best every day.

Move out into the world with excitement and curiosity so that each day is a big day for you.

7. Nostalgia for the past

Too many people live in the past and I have written about this in many of my books. This leads to loneliness since you separate yourself from what you are now, and from your life situation and your world of today.

Perhaps your past was better than your present; perhaps you are just deluding yourself when you think it was. In either case you cannot live today as if it were yesterday; this is as unrealistic as drinking water and telling yourself it is champagne. Children, play-acting, can do this; as an adult you must put the games of childhood behind and face the often harsh and demanding aspects of your reality.

When you keep longing for the past, and living in the past, pulling yourself back into the past, you do injury to your sense of reality. You betray a lack of faith in your ability to stand up to the stresses of life, you surrender your maturity to illusion.

Once again let us flip the coin. From NOSTALGIA FOR THE PAST to THE PRESENT.

Today is your day to live.

Help yourself enjoy your day.

Encourage your positive qualities today.

Prepare for a day of confidence and achievement.

Resist negative feelings that would destroy your good day.

Eliminate yesterday's failures: today is your day.

See your good goals for today.

Evoke your positive qualities; today life goes on.

Nourish your enthusiasm of the now.

Try to get to your better self today.

8. Enslavement

Those were wretched days for human beings, when some privileged people made slaves of other people. And, in the dubious pages of history, we find other horrifying examples of enslavement and imprisonment, such as the unimaginably brutal enslavement and massacre of millions of human beings in Germany's concentration camps.

These external forms of enslavement are nightmarish, oppressive forces militating against any reasonable attempts of so many people to live happy, constructive lives—and of course we condemn them.

And yet, what do we do—with ourselves? Is it not true that millions of us enslave ourselves? Is it not true that millions of us force ourselves into concentration camps we have built in our minds, denying ourselves sunshine and light? Is it not true that millions of us, kind to others at least superficially, have enslaved ourselves in ignorance and dissociation, betraying ourselves?

We must resolve not to enslave ourselves into loneliness. We must become creative mind watchers, constantly on the alert for the negative forces within ourselves that would undermine us, constantly seeking to find the good in ourselves.

A story about enslavement—about a young man in his early twenties, enslaved to loneliness, to resentment, to despair—and to sleep.

His appearance did not inspire confidence. Sloppy clothes. Unshaven. Indifferent manner.

He told me about his life. For years he slept during the day. Day after day he slept and slept. He stayed up all night, got his sleep during the day. He did this, he told me, to get revenge on his father, who had dominated him all his life and who treated him like an "eight-year-old." His mother had died when he was eight and since then he had lived with his father, aunt and uncle in a two-family house. His aunt and uncle picked on him all the time, he complained, and his father bossed him around. He had long missed his mother, had broken down for three years after her death. And he had failed in school for years.

"Anyway," he said, "I sleep during the day. I stay up all night and I sleep during the day."

Obviously he was enslaved to an extremely unfortunate past—and to sleep.

How could I help him?

"You have to give yourself another chance," I told him. "You are worth it. We all deserve another chance."

"If I could only change."

"Maybe you can—if you learn to forget the griefs of the past and live in the present."

"That's easy to say."

"Maybe so," I said. "But you have to know this: You can't bring your mother back. Her death must have hurt you terribly, but you must go on in spite of your grief and live in the present. You must break your enslavement to the past—and to sleep—and to negation and loneliness. You must live today, you must fight for your right to live, not sleep your life away."

Shrink from ENSLAVEMENT; move instead toward PARTICIPATION. In doing so, you move from loneliness to happiness.

Practice belonging to a world that may not be perfect, but that is the only world you've got.

Accept yourself as the person you are, and don't try to imitate someone else.

Remember the compassion in you that can make you free.

Turn toward others with friendliness.

Investigate the good in others, but first examine the good in yourself.

Concentrate on your goals.

Insist on fair play.

Plan forward, liberating movement toward people.

Aspire for good; this will free you.

Tackle life's problems without fear of mistakes and you will be bursting your chains.

Instill in your heart your desire to give, not just to take, and you will feel liberated and powerful.

Opportunity beckons if you see it; look for it and take advantage of it.

Never shirk your responsibility to yourself to unlock your true personality and live a full life.

9. Selfishness

One thing must be clear to you: You must be of great value to yourself and you must give up first place in your own mind to no one.

Still, when an individual thinks of himself to the exclusion of all others, he is isolating himself from others—and, in a way, from himself—and plunging himself into a state of loneliness.

When an individual acts solely out of selfishness, never thinking of others, he automatically becomes just a taker in life, never a giver, and in the long run he will find himself alone and taking away from himself, too. The truly selfish person does not play ball; he must make up all the rules and be the entire ball game—and other people will not play with him.

And what is the other side of SELFISHNESS? That's right, PLAYING BALL.

Preparation for genuine self-improvement starts with playing ball with yourself and extends outward to playing ball with others.

Let go your feelings of resentment; when you do, you are playing ball with yourself.

Achieving a goal implies sharing it with others and then moving from loneliness to happiness.

Your recognition of your real worth is the beginning of your mature acceptance of yourself and of others.

Imagine yourself as you are in your best moments, and project this better you out into a world of improving human relations and happiness.

No more scathing self-criticism means that you are playing ball with yourself and defeating loneliness.

Giving, not taking, is how to play ball.

Being true to yourself is the beginning of being true to others, and the entire process represents movement away from loneliness to creative living.

Attempting to rise above negative feelings implies more growth.

Live creatively today; this is playing ball.

Look at yourself kindly, and your loneliness is on the run.

10. Separation

Throughout history we find people known as Separatists who, because of one controversy or another—as in England centuries ago—split themselves off from the main branch of a religious body or government to more independently espouse heartfelt views about the relevant issues.

But we will discuss separation from a different point of view: in terms of the individual's separation from his self-image, and from the world of people.

And, indeed, all the components of loneliness that we have discussed involve, in one way or another, separation.

You must practice honesty. If you are honest with yourself, then you need not deceive yourself, you keep your personality intact, accessible to you.

You will then feel no need to hide from other people, or to fool other people—because you accept yourself—except under specially extenuating circumstances.

Less separate from your self-image, less separate from others, you will suffer less from loneliness.

Now, once again, let's turn the coin over. Turn—and we will find BELONGING.

Believe in your contribution to others.

Engage in constructive programs with others.

Let your imagination work creatively for you, and for others, as you plan meaningful goals.

Object to factors which separate you from others.

Neglect of self-esteem will result in isolation.

Go forward confidently, as if you belong, and chances are you will belong.

Invest your sincerity and your loyalty in others. This will bring you closer to them.

Never force your view on other people.

Give other people a chance. Try to talk less, and listen more.

YOUR PAST LONELINESS

And so we have *spelled out* loneliness for you. And then, as a counterforce, we have spelled out the positive forces, the forces that will move you away from loneliness to happiness.

Do you look forward to moving day? I mean the day when the moving van comes and your dishes are in crates and your books are tied up in bundles and so on. Do you like moving day?

I must confess that I do not like it, that I

like to be comfortable and settled. Most people, I imagine, also feel this way.

Still, one moving day you must truly look forward to: the day you move from loneliness to happiness. This is the move you must make—to greener pastures, to bluer skies, to sunnier lands with fresher air. Your rent will remain the same, and you will tax yourself less. Yes, this is a move you must make.

And then, as you build your self-image and set your goals, as you reactivate your success mechanism and practice the soothing balm of forgiveness, as you forget your past mistakes and let your successes live in technicolor in the wonderful world of your imagination, then, as your days grow brighter and you face each day with resurgent pleasantness, as you smile at the new day and plan it lovingly, then you will find you are concretizing your position in this new land: HAPPINESS.

And then your loneliness will be in the past. You will feel it no longer; you will think of it no longer; it will no longer obsess you.

You will then no longer talk of loneliness as a present reality, but as a past reality. You will refer to it as your *past loneliness*, you will leave it in the past as you live constructively in the present.

CREATIVE MIND WATCHING

We wind up our discussion of self-fulfillment with this chapter on creative mind watching.

We have spelled out for you a number of helpful concepts, including the overcoming of conscience as a negative force, the value of self-acceptance, the storehouse of power in your imagination, and the importance of setting and reaching out to achieve goals.

Now, finally, we will spell out for you the ingredients of creative mind watching.

But, first, what do we mean by mind watching?

The words are self-explanatory. The mind watcher focuses where it counts—on the operation of his thinking-imaging processes. Creatively he guards against negative thoughts and images while looking to cement positive thoughts and images. The bird watcher looks for creatures that interest him; the creative mind watcher looks for springboards to emotional growth and self-fulfillment that are absolutely essential for him.

The creative mind watcher turns ideas into performance. He does this every day that he can and, doing so, strengthens his self-image and oils the gears of his success mechanism and marches toward self-fulfillment.

Today's television watcher is often a passive individual whose only active role may be flicking the dial on his set when he is displeased with what he is watching.

But today's creative mind watcher is active. Mind watching first, emotional growth next, and finally an active movement out into the world in pursuit of goals with which an individual finds self-fulfillment.

And now suppose that we turn to the spelling out of MIND WATCHERS.

THE GROWTH WORLD OF THE MIND WATCHERS

This takes us into a growth world; mind watchers want no dull status quo. They want improvement. They want satisfaction. And they insist on reaching self-fulfillment.

1. **M** Molding the Better You.
2. **I** Imaginative Power.
3. **N** No Negative Feelings.
4. **D** Determination to Reach Goals.

5. **W** Why not be a Winner in Life?
6. **A** Action, Trying, Doing.
7. **T** Today Is the Day.
8. **C** Compassion, Courage, Concentration.
9. **H** Habits that Work.
10. **E** Enthusiastic Excitement.
11. **R** Relaxation Plus.
12. **S** Success as a Way of Life.

That's MIND WATCHERS, spelled out for you. Now let's see what they mean.

1. Molding the better you

You mold the better you only when you get to know yourself, realistically, and when you accept your faults even while you minimize their total impact, yet build on your virtues which give you body and character as a person.

You refuse to practice evasion. You find yourself free to mold the better you when you look into your mirror truthfully. As you look into your mirror, seeing yourself superficially and yet with depth, you forgive yourself for yesterday's errors and you applaud yourself for the successes of today and tomorrow.

You see a complicated, composite truth about yourself—not a make-believe truth of pretense—and you accept this multi-dimensional truth.

It is, then, out of reality that you build the better you, looking straight ahead, not hiding your head in the sand. You emphasize the strong points in yourself that you see, realistically, and thus you give meaning to the better side of yourself.

2. Imaginative power

This power is not electric, it is not atomic—it is merely the great human power.

As a creative mind watcher, you keep an eye on your imagination.

You refuse to let images of doom and catastrophe take root there, filling your entire personality with a sense of failure.

You refuse to let images of your past blunders take root there, preconditioning you to more failure—in a depressing cycle that never ends and never turns upward.

You refuse to allow irrelevancy and distortion to take over the rambling inner space of your imagination.

Your imagination is not a wasteland for trespassing negation and you hang out a sign which reads NO TRESPASSING when the destructive side of yourself tries to inhabit this rich and fertile area.

You use your imagination constructively.

Making imagination your friend, you see there your past successes, and you build the good past into the good present as you move toward the good life.

Imagination is the eye of creative mind watchers who see within to what they can be and, inspired, rise to the opportunity to build meaningful lives for themselves.

Let me tell you a story about a very brave man, who insisted on fighting oppressive forces to forget a horrible past and find a worthwhile present.

His past? "They lined us up against a wall —over one hundred of us—and then they mowed us down with machine guns."

This man wanted me to operate on him. I looked at him—he was in his late forties, short, blue eyes, graying blond hair—and wondered how he had survived that concentration camp in Germany in 1944.

"I was wounded in the face here—in the jaw and neck. My friends who rescued me put a piece of rug against the bleeding wound; they hid me in the concentration camp. The rest, all dead and buried en masse in a deep wide hole in the ground." He paused as if to see again in his mind those horrible events.

"The months passed. I had fever and I thought I would die. Many days I can't remember what happened. All I know is that somehow I survived. And then the American soldiers came."

He looked at the floor. Then, after a deep

breath, "My mother, father, sisters, brothers—all gone. I traveled all over the world. But I could not forget."

He wiped his eyes and his wife whom he had married a year ago put her arm around him. "Do you think you could help, doctor?" she asked.

"Maybe. Why did you wait so long? It is twenty-five years since it happened."

"I wasn't ready."

"I don't understand."

"You see, I wanted to remember. I didn't want to forget. It was comforting to remember the past —before those terrible times—when things were all right and we were happy."

"And you're ready now?"

"Yes, I am."

I studied his face. A deep indented scar on the right side under the chin distorted it terribly— it was as if he were two people, one handsome, the other distorted.

"I want to forget," he said. "I want a new start, a new life."

I told him I would operate and that I would also remove the tattoo numbers on his arm.

It was a rather difficult operation, but when I finished the results were splendid. His face was symmetrical again.

I had operated under local anesthesia. "Finished," I said.

Then he made a request. "Can I take a look?"

In approximately forty-five years of plastic surgery, having performed something like twenty thousand operations, I had never heard such a request at such a moment.

I took my gloves off and handed him a mirror. He studied himself at length, then whispered, "Thanks, doctor, thanks."

A week later, the final stitches were removed

and the stitches on his arm. He looked at his face. He beamed with satisfaction. All he said was "Thanks," but the look on his face told me that, in spite of all the agonies of his past, he had wiped them from his imagination and was living in the present. Freed from the past, he was a new person—a person he once had been.

He gave me a present before he left. It was a rag doll. That is his business. He manufactures dolls and ships them all over North and South America.

That night I thought about this brave man who refused to allow his imagination to remain a wasteland of negation, who insisted on escaping from his nightmarish memories and on using the power of his imagination for creative living in the present.

3. No negative feelings

The creative mind watcher is constantly on the lookout for negative feelings. He is so attuned to his self-protective task that he can feel negative feelings moving in on him; he can almost smell and taste them. He guards himself from his own negative feelings as desperately as a bank would guard itself against robbers and, indeed, this is a good comparison since negative feelings would rob him of his inner peace.

No negative feelings. No negative feelings because they hold you back from your real self.

This does not mean that you reject yourself for your weaknesses.

Not at all. You accept them, you live with them—and you rise above them.

You learn to live with your mistakes—and you learn to rise above your mistakes. Then—and only then—is your self-image solid, made of muscle—not papier-mâché.

Still, you aspire toward positive ways of thinking and imaging and doing.

If you own a house, you may take advantage of Grievance Day and on this day you may register an objection to the assessment if you feel it is unfair or inaccurate or whatever. And perhaps a reviewing board, considering your case, may agree that your grievance is valid and may change your situation so that your effort was worthwhile.

This is a positive way to register your grievances—it is if your contentions are valid, anyway.

But getting away from home owning and real estate matters to grievances in general, too many people use grievances as a way of life. Every day to them is Grievance Day. Every day they submerge themselves in negative feelings. Every day they wallow in self-pity, feel themselves deprived, and complain to other people who don't really listen.

Escape from grievances that never end and all negative feelings that never end. Escape to an imagination that sees—if not green pastures—a life that is worthwhile in a world that, though troubled, contains heartwarming compensations for those who choose to open their eyes and see them.

I've already written at great length about my father. He looked upon neighborhood grievances as opportunites for gentle, friendly arbitration. He liked to help his neighbors with their troubles.

Do this for yourself. Help yourself with your troubles. Defend yourself against your grievances, when they are unrealistically dominating and when they obsess you. Be a good neighbor to yourself.

How do you do this?

By creative mind watching. By watching out for the first signs that you are sabotaging yourself and then moving to eliminate these invasions of negative feelings.

4. Determination to reach goals

Often, in my travels, I hear people complain that they have "no desire," that they have "no goals."

I do not fully believe them when they say this. If there is one thing that is common to all human beings, I believe it is the determination to live and to be happy. This is our paramount goal.

Branching off from this main goal are many subordinate goals and in our determination to achieve these goals and in the constructive efforts with which we implement our determination, we reach our full stature as human beings. Each day we recharge our batteries and start off on new adventures in pursuit of new goals.

Let me tell you about one woman and her goal.

She attended a seminar in psycho-cybernetics. A married woman in her forties—her two children were married—she came from a well-to-do family, but she felt she was going nowhere with herself. She needed movement, a goal; she needed to find her ability.

Finally, she did find herself. She became a real estate agent in a small community in California; she was determined to be a success in her occupation. And she did succeed. She stuck to her goal of success in her field, and she achieved her goal.

At the end of the seminar she came over to talk to me and she told me just how great she felt.

Of course she did. She mobilized her determination to reach her goal, and she made it.

The creative mind watcher will feel this determination to reach his goals. He will creatively steer his thinking to productive goals, and then he will proceed to go after them with determination.

5. Why not be a winner in life?

If you are a creative mind watcher, you have a real chance because, like Babe Ruth, you keep your eye on the ball and you keep thinking of hitting "home runs."

You work to develop in your life extensions of your past successes and entirely new successes. As a creative mind watcher, you are always on the alert for the blossoming of success feelings in your imagination.

It is easy to tell yourself that you are an unlucky person and that you never get a break, but let's face it: you have to make your breaks.

In an earlier chapter I told you the story of two people in their sixties—a man and a woman —who seemed doomed to lives of boredom. And yet, in their sixties, when so many people are concretizing already rigid routines, these two old-young people found in themselves a winning spirit.

If they can do it, why not you?

You begin with creative mind watching; you end with positive action.

6. Action, trying, doing

To be a creative mind watcher you must act, try, do. You think positively, then you do positively.

You do more than regulate the thermostat of your mind. You then take the constructive thinking processes you have arranged in your mind and you bring the full weight of them out into action.

A friend of mine told me about infantry combat during World War II in Europe. They were near the French-German border and his division was advancing day after day. Their casualties had been brutally heavy; he was one of the few left alive. So he was first scout and he walked far ahead of the body of his outfit as they walked from village to village. He was always vigilant—he had to be in his exposed position—and as an American he was always watching, watching, watching all the area in front for signs of the German enemy.

As a creative mind watcher, you must be just as vigilant. For your enemy. The enemy that would destroy you as Hitler, if he could have, would have destroyed us.

The enemy? Negative feelings.

7. Today is the day

Action, trying, doing. Fine. But when?

Today. Today is the time for your self-fulfillment. Today is the time for your adventure in living.

Not tomorrow. Today.

As a creative mind watcher, you insist on your being a full, independent person. You will not let others dominate and enslave your thinking.

You are in your automobile, heading for your destination. You are in the driver's seat, and you will let nobody else drive your car. *You* are the driver. And, when you come to a dead end, you back up, turn around, and resume your journey toward your goal.

Victor Hugo believed that a timely idea was more important than all the armed might of the world.

Well, here's a timely idea for you: Become a mind watcher and guide yourself to the good life today.

For today is the day.

8. Compassion, courage, concentration

According to the philosopher Schopenhauer, compassion is the basis of morality.

How true!

For compassion implies a dedication to your fellow man that underlies the desire of people to band together in communities. And it underlies the morality with which they try to live together.

This type of compassion takes courage because, vulnerable as we have been all our lives to even the suggestion that others have slighted us or taken advantage of us, we need courage to rise above these real or imagined wrongs to feel compassionate fellow-feelings for our brothers and sisters.

This is an underrated form of courage: it can involve more genuine daring than many heralded feats on battlefield or athletic field. It is unfortunate but true that not too many people seem courageous enough to practice compassion as a way of life. When you do, however, you will find how much giving to others will give to you.

As a mind watcher, you exercise concentration as you develop your capacities for compassion and courage. Concentration is a fine art; you screen out of your mind the static that would interrupt the beautiful music; you filter out of your mind the irrelevancies that would leave you a passive slave—not the master—of your thoughts.

In exercising concentration, you are selective and you choose to focus on the building of qualities that will help your self-image grow and lead you toward self-fulfillment—qualities such as compassion and courage.

9. Habits that work

The creative mind watcher is on the lookout for the habits he forms and the habits he is able to discard.

For we all have habits that work and at the same time habits that do not work.

Brushing your teeth in the morning, this habit works. It works because you're better off for having this habit. As a result of it, your mouth may be a happier part of you, refreshed perhaps, better smelling perhaps, and in better shape for breakfast.

Or take another habit that will work for you —tying your shoelaces after you put on your shoes. You don't often think twice about this, you just do it, and if you didn't you'd probably spend half your time tripping over yourself.

Some habits, however, do not work for you. Too much drinking or too much smoking is a simple example—so is overeating. On an interpersonal level, you may have developed the unworkable habit of disputing anything a friend says, interrupting him before he can finish saying it. Needless to say, if you have this habit, your friendships will be stormy and, if your friendships last, it is fair to say that you have tolerant friends (or friends who are also extremely argumentative).

Anyway, habits that do not work—what do you do about them?

Well, what would you do about any intruder —or any intruding force—that injured the caliber of your life?

Cockroaches, for example. What would you do if a huge group of cockroaches embedded themselves in the crevices lining your apartment?

You'd call the exterminator?

That sounds like par for the course.

And your negative thinking habits? How about exterminating them, too? With creative mind watching.

For when you are a creative mind watcher, you stand guard over your imagination and you guard it, like a sentinel, against the enemy that creeps up on you in the night, ready to invade, ready to capture you. You stand ready to rout the forces of this enemy—negative feelings.

Repel your habits that are negative and do not work; encourage your habits that are positive and that will work for you.

And the thing to remember is this: Though your habits, by definition, may be strongly entrenched, you can do battle with them.

Heed the example of Mr. H., who was able to discard deeply embedded patterns of boring park-benchmanship and a listless routine that never varied to move on into a new life of adventure and possibility. Mr. H., if you'll remember, needed a dog to jolt him out of his dull habits; maybe you can do it all by yourself.

10. Enthusiastic excitement

As a creative mind watcher, enthusiastic excitement is one of your goals. You weed out of your mind the nonsense that you must be stodgy and poker-faced—because of your age, perhaps, or your social position or whatever—and you allow yourself, and encourage, a curiosity in seeking new adventures and an enthusiasm and excitement for what each day will bring.

Your day begins when you wake up in the morning and shake off the grogginess, overcome the impulses toward negative feelings and vow to make this day exciting.

Your day will not be an exercise in inertia;

you have goals and you have more than enthusiasm for them.

These goals excite you.

Even if you are in your retirement years and people say you should be bored and sit around doing nothing, you ignore this silly advice. You feel enthusiasm for the goals of your day; they excite you.

Even if you are having a rough time—for the time being you are under great external pressure and the breaks are not going your way—you set goals for your day with excitement. For this is a new day; you will bring new hope to your new day. The defeats of the last few days or weeks or months belong to yesterday, and you will forget them.

Excitement can be plus or minus. Excitement minus means you have no goals and, in your negative state, fear and anxiety set in. But excitement plus means you feel enthusiasm for your goals and an urgency to reach them. Your basic goal is to fulfill yourself. Start from there, and move toward excitement plus.

Let even little things give you delight.

The other day, for example, I was walking down Fifth Avenue in New York—I was with a friend—and a woman rushed up to me and seized my hand, shaking hands with me. "Hello," she said.

"Hello," I said.

"How are you?" she said.

"Fine. How are you?"

"It's been wonderful running into you," she said. "I'm sorry but I'm late for an appointment." Away she went.

I felt pleased at this pleasant little interlude —even though as I walked on with my friend, I kept wondering, *Who is she?*

And you. Give enthusiasm to all these little, unimportant parts of life.

You'll feel better for it.

11. Relaxation plus

Excitement plus—relaxation plus; a good followup. For there is no genuine fulfillment without relaxation; it doesn't matter what mountains you have climbed if you are not able to relax. No goal-striving is truly worthwhile if you cannot give yourself the chance to recuperate and renew your powers now and then.

We are human beings, not supermen. Perhaps supermen can keep driving twenty-four hours a day, I don't know. What I do know is that flesh-and-blood human beings cannot keep up such a pace.

Many years ago, long before any of us were born, worldly wise Benjamin Franklin compared people who could rest to those who could take cities and found that the ones who could relax were greater.

And, more placidly, the poet Wordsworth referred to "the universal instinct of repose, the longing for confirmed tranquility."

Marvelous recommendations for the power of relaxation from men of wisdom.

The creative mind watcher is on the lookout for signs of fatigue. Aware that he has limitations and that recognition of these limitations is a strength, not a weakness, he knows when to stop driving and start relaxing.

When he starts relaxing, he commits himself wholeheartedly to it—no half-and-half thing. Just as he moves with all his power toward the implementation of his goals, so he throws himself wholeheartedly into relaxation. He feels that he has earned his rest because he has lived fully, with enthusiasm and excitement, with determination and desire. So now he can accept the idea of relaxation. He can let himself go limp; his mind can rest and his body can rest. And this is what I call relaxation plus.

With relaxation plus I don't know if you can conquer cities (what with urban problems these days you might not even want to) but, if you would believe Ben Franklin, you are in good shape.

Some suggestion for the attainment of relaxation plus:

A. *Practice forgiveness.* Forgive others; they are only human. Forgive yourself; you too are only human. When you hold grudges, you *may* hurt the other fellow, but you *must* hurt yourself with the accumulated poison of the resentment you feel inside you. The individual who does not forgive does not really live.

When you forgive others, you take one giant step toward relaxation plus. When you forgive yourself, you are there.

B. *Keep up with yourself.* Forget about keeping up with your next-door neighbor or the neighbor down the block. When you worry about keeping up with others, you are not living in your own right; you are a slave to whatever rules these "others" wish to impose upon you—and isn't this silly?

A more legitimate goal is to keep up with yourself, and even to surpass yourself—as each day you aim at becoming a more fully mature, more productive, more compassionate person. Here *you* make up the rules of the game.

C. *See your past successes.* See them again and again in your powerhouse: your imagination. Stop the flow of tension you feel as you obsess yourself with your blunders and your missteps; see instead in your mind your past successes so that you can relax with this good feeling about yourself.

12. Success as a way of life

This is a fundamental concept of the creative mind watcher. He is alert to the incipient reactivations of his failure mechanism and his success mechanism. His aim is to steer himself toward success—as a way of life. He does everything he can to keep from being trapped in the quicksand of failure.

The creative mind watcher, taking dead aim on success, works to strengthen his self-image.

He sees himself at his best—realistically, but taking a positive approach.

He understands his rights as a goal-striving human being. This involves refusing to feel inferior to other people. He does not feel inferior to celebrities or to heads of governments or to business tycoons. He acknowledges their talents, their channelized aggressiveness, their manipulative abilities, their confidence, all their assets. But still he does not feel inferior to them; they are human beings and he is a human being. Every day he does his best and that is good enough for him. He is inferior to nobody; God has created him as a unique individual with rights.

He sets goals for himself, goals that are realistic and inspiring. After he sets his goals, he works out strategies for achieving them and then moves out toward them. Failure and frustration do not stop him because there is always a new day and with the new day he renews his goal-striving.

Strengthening his self-image, making positive use of his imagination, recognizing his human rights, and moving on his goals, he reactivates the functioning of his success mechanism and comes to live a life of success.

The successful way of life; you must make this your way of life.

MIND WATCHING AND SELF-FULFILLMENT

And so we have completed our voyage into the growth world of the creative mind watchers.

This is a growth world because creative mind watchers are aware of human possibilities. They are fortunate people in that, in this complex and confusing world with its overwhelming barrage of distractions, they know where to look for real human satisfactions.

Creative mind watchers do not lose themselves along the many by-roads that lead to loneliness and desolation; they are too aware of genuine human values and they understand that the main highway—even in a civilization in turmoil—leads to the warmth of human friendship. Friendship, a beautiful word, but not an abstraction. Friendship—first for oneself, then for others.

This is why you, participating with me in this little discussion we've had in these pages, should be a creative mind watcher. A truly creative mind watcher, who turns inward for your strength, then outward with your strength to live purposefully in a world you should not give up on.

Then you are on your way to self-fulfillment.

With a strong self-image.

Setting goals that are real.

Overcoming the potential tyrannny of conscience.

Using your imagination as a potent force for good.

A final word of advice: *You can reach self-fulfillment; it is an honest possibility.*

I say this because so many people these days

hold their heads in their hands and moan about how horrible the world is, how inhumane, how bestial, how cold and indifferent. I say this because so many people shake their heads from side to side and moan about the speed of change in modern life, about the lack of faith and trust, about the horrors of the nuclear bomb and the nuclear age. I say this because so many people, after a quick glance at the newspaper headlines and a minute or two in front of the television set watching the news, are ready to give up on the world and dive under their blankets to hide.

The world is an admittedly difficult place often, I will agree, and I don't always like what's going on any more than you do.

Still, I will repeat: Self-fulfillment is a possibility in this world; it is not an empty goal.

You move toward it by strengthening your inner resources along the lines that I have suggested.

And you, reading my words, I hope that I have helped you to make self-fulfillment not a meaningless abstraction—but an actuality.

PART TWO

QUESTIONS AND ANSWERS

For years now, people have been asking me questions about my theory of psycho-cybernetics: people who have read my book *Psycho-Cybernetics,* or *The Magic Power of Self-Image Psychology* or *Creative Living for Today;* people who have attended my lectures throughout the country; people who are interested in improving the quality of their lives.

I have jotted down their questions from time to time and here are some of them, with my answers. I hope you'll find them helpful.

For easier reading, I have broken down these questions and answers in terms of subject matter and then arranged them alphabetically. There is, of course, some overlap (many may branch off into two or more different areas), but I feel this system will aid you in locating the specific subject matter that interests you most.

ANGER

Q. Anger—sudden and often—why? Is it necessary? If not vented will it cause frustration?
A. Anger is one of the great destructive forces

within us that hurts us most when we give vent to it. It comes sudden and often because you give it life.

Is it necessary? No. But life without it, without resentment, negative feelings is no life at all. Perhaps these negative feelings come our way as red lights telling us to stop, look, and listen—take stock of ourselves, remember our assets, know that we can rise above anger.

Can you picture self-respect with anger? Humility, with anger? Compassion? Self-acceptance?

Unlikely. Anger *is* frustration, an explosive kind of frustration in which you turn a passive feeling of hurt into an active performance of willful destruction.

How does one overcome anger?

Each person must find his own way by remembering that the world within him is part failure, part success—and success means the capacity to rise above failure and above anger.

Here are three ways of standing up to anger:

1. Look in the mirror. See your face in anger, the snarling expression. Now turn this face into your other face, the one of confidence with a smile on it. The first tension, the second relaxation. Ask yourself how long you want to be angry. Make the decision and see if you have the courage to laugh, then laugh out loud.

2. Get rid of the pent-up energies in some activity—even walking. Walk, walk, walk. Forgive, forgive, forgive. Forgive others and yourself.

3. Write the nastiest letter you can with all those words you want to use; write it as long as you want it to be, then read it and re-read it (and you have just passed through a decompression chamber you have created for yourself). Then tear up the letter and throw it into a wastepaper basket.

QUESTIONS AND ANSWERS

COMPASSION

Q. My daughter age three asked me the following question: What is the nicest word?
A. I asked this question of many people in my lectures throughout the country and invariably the answer would be: *love.*

I would answer by saying that *compassion* is the nicest word because it incorporates love.

Compassion also means the giving of your courage to someone else; it means your optimism about life, your maturity, the transplantation of some of your assurance to someone else; it means your self-confidence, self-acceptance and self-respect, shared with others; it means the sharing of your ingenuity for positive creative action with others and the transplanting of your nucleus of faith into others. Compassion is a full-time job that needs no time. It is the beginning of the brotherhood of man. With it you are *somebody.* Without it you are *nothing.*

It is ironic that Schopenhauer who hated mankind said that "Compassion is the basis of all morality." How true!

One evening after a lecture in a church in Seattle, Washington, one young man of 17 asked this question: "Suppose you had to leave this world in the next hour. What advice can you give in one sentence to us young people?"

I answered quickly: "I don't need a sentence. I can give it to you in one word—COMPASSION."

When you have compassion, you are expressing humility, the greatest trait of the success instinct within you. The world then belongs to you for you know that the world belongs to all other human beings, too. You share your fortune with

175

others, you share love of mankind with others. You express the God-like quality within you.

And you cannot give compassion to others unless you have compassion for yourself. Don't ever sell yourself short. Have *compassion*.

DISCIPLINE

Q. What is discipline?
A. In Vienna about one hundred years ago many women died in the hospital after giving birth. A Professor Klein claimed it was a pollution from the atmosphere. A young doctor, Philip Semmelweis, didn't believe this and finally discovered childbed fever was blood poisoning brought about by contamination from the hands of medical students who had examined the women. Professor Klein represented authority. Semmelweis represented freedom of thought and truth. Authority kicked Semmelweis out of the hospital. He spent the rest of his life fighting for his ideas, but authority was deaf. Finally, examining a tissue specimen of a mother dead from childbed fever, Semmelweis cut his finger accidently, developed a fever and died. Even though a man, he got childbed fever. Thus, even in tragedy, freedom of thought triumphed over authority.

In the household we find another battle between authority and freedom of thought: parental authority versus freedom of expression for children.

Children have the future on their side; adults have maturity and wisdom on theirs. Still, parental authority is ill advised when it involves punishment and lack of understanding.

Discipline of a child must be creative, not destructive, as in Dr. Klein's punishment of Dr.

Semmelweis. Indeed, it is more a test of the adult than of the child. Understanding and self-respect are keys to creative discipline.

Creative discipline is a partnership between parent and child, a board meeting between the self-image of an adult who has made mistakes and that of a youngster who will make mistakes. In creating this companionable atmosphere, discipline is constructive. The adult still has his self-respect; so has the child.

Thus discipline can only be creative if it first involves self-discipline: control of emotions that lead us to fail—fear, anger—use of emotions that help us—understanding, self-respect, courage. We cannot impose our self-image on a child; the child has his own self-image. We must help him improve his self-image and be happy with it.

Creative discipline in industry is also a partnership: between the parent—the manager—and his children—the managed. There must be a psychological meeting of the minds—a board meeting—with respect and compassion.

EMOTIONAL SCARS

Q. Have you a simple guide to heal emotional scars?
A. I wouldn't call this a "simple" guide, but you can heal your emotional scars. If you don't sell yourself out.

If you don't keep bemoaning your "bad luck" or hiding because you feel you're unworthy.

In terms of emotional scars, American Negroes have realistically legitimate grievances. And though we may point to progress, basic inequities remain.

Yet these people endured—with emotional

177

scars, true, but they endured. And, surely, they felt a great pride in their ability to keep going under such trying conditions.

As did the Jewish survivors of the horrifying Hitler persecution, who, arriving here with families and possessions gone, gritted their teeth and built a new life.

Or the persons who, born in poverty or with other disadvantages, have fought their way to their goals.

Learn a lesson from such people who refused to let emotional scars disfigure them.

Forget about your "bad luck" or "unworthiness." Question your feeling that you are inferior.

When your frustrations enrage you, channel your feeling. Use it constructively in your own interests.

And every day ask yourself: How do I, my own plastic surgeon, heal my emotional wounds?

Your best tool is the self-image you create. You create this picture of yourself when you rise above blunders and turn crises into opportunities. *You* create this strong image of yourself.

EVIL

Q. You said that you do not recognize "evil." In the Old Testament the Lord says "I created evil." Are you not closing your eyes to reality? How can we, as you suggest, completely ignore one of the great forces in this world—the force for good and the force for evil? Shouldn't we know our enemy?
A. In the first place I didn't say that. I said that to me the greatest evil in man is within himself when he makes a blunder and refuses to rise above it. As I mentioned in my book, there are two forces within us; the will to survive and the will to self-

destruction: the will for happiness and the will for unhappiness; the will to succeed and the will to fail. We have a success mechanism within us and a failure mechanism within us—our assets, our liabilities. And we learn about the failure instinct within us only to see what it is so that we can rise above it by using our confidence, courage, and understanding. Living creatively means not just being successful, but being successful by rising above a blunder.

The greatest evil, I repeat, is to complain about a failure and do nothing about rising above it. When I said you should turn your back on negative feelings and live creatively today by using your confidence to reach a goal in the present, I didn't mean that you shouldn't recognize negative feelings, but the reverse. Recognize them, but do more than that. Do something creative with them by turning a crisis into an opportunity.

EXISTENTIALISM

Q. What is the relationship between psycho-cybernetics and existentialism?
A. I spoke at a seminar in Encino, California, last year and one person congratulated me on my book saying it was a remarkable work on existentialism. I didn't know what he meant.

Which reminds me of the time when I was addressing a group of sales executives in Miami Beach. I entered the 9th floor elevator ready to meet friends in the lobby, when I overheard a young girl of 18 not knowing who I was, say to her boyfriend of 22:

"I don't like psycho-cybernetics."

"I do," the man answered. "Why don't you like it?"

"It isn't vague enough," she replied. "I like Sartre, he's vague."

In the first place there is nothing vague about Sartre, the great exponent of existentialism. His play *No Exit* expresses his philosophy. It is a philosophy of negation, has a negative connotation, that there is no future, no hope for man; that he is the victim of a futility syndrome.

Psycho-cybernetics is just the reverse, expressing hope and belief in man and the conviction that he himself has the power within him to fulfill himself and raise himself to his full stature of self-respect and dignity as a human being. We are not talking about "no exits." We are talking about "entrances," entrances into creative living that we determine within ourselves. Existentialism is a red light! STOP. Psycho-cybernetics is a green light: GO FORWARD to your goal.

There is an old Irish proverb: "If God shuts one door He opens another." We can paraphrase that by saying that if man shuts one door upon successful living because he failed in one undertaking, he must be ready with his hand on the knob to open up another door of opportunity to succeed. He is Opportunity and when he succeeds he expresses the God-like quality within him.

FRIENDSHIP

Q. What is friendship?
A. Friendship is something most of us seek to attain, but many of us become disappointed in its results. We find ourselves disappointed in others, we feel wounded and maltreated. We seldom wonder if *we* had been at fault. It must have been the other person.

Friendship is a most important undertaking

in our lives. It is a basic goal. We must try to understand it more.

For friendship is not what we take from others, but what we give. It is instilling courage in someone else. It is the transfer of our self-respect to others. It is the sharing of our confidence with others. It is the gift of what we are to others.

In friendship, we offer part of ourselves to others to grow to our proper stature of fulfillment.

We must remember others, meet others more than half way, giving our best selves to others. Only thus do we receive friendship in return.

We must be constantly busy repairing our self-image. For to be a friend to others, you must first be a friend to yourself. You must always be ready to repair the damage you inflict on yourself if you do not accept your failures. You must rise above these failures to accept yourself. Only then can you give your friendship to others, and only then can it have true value.

Q. How do you make friends?
A. I'll tell you about four women I know who meet once a week, every Friday evening. They rotate their meetings at each other's apartments. They have been meeting Friday evenings for about thirty years. They were quite young when they first met and all four had natural blonde hair. So they had the color of their hair in common.

But they had something much more in common, too. They were unable to hide their feelings. And when these four young women first met, they immediately became friends.

The years have passed and the women are in their sixties. They are more devoted to each other than ever.

But what do they do on Friday evenings? They discuss their families, the news, new fashions, and new plays and movies. But the really important business of these evenings is—poker.

The women are devoted poker players.

A devoted poker player bets money, of course, and they bet money. Not big sums, but not tiny, either.

And here is the startling thing:

At the end of each year, the four women wind up even. Because they still have not learned to conceal their feelings. None can assume a "poker face." When one gets an excellent hand, her eyes light up. When another has some luck, she utters a little sound of pleasure. The third woman smiles, and the fourth beams.

Are these amateurish card players? Perhaps. But, in another way, I think they are fortunate. For they enjoy themselves and remain friends, because they *don't know how to put on a poker face*.

Anyway, the question is How to make—and how to *keep*—friends.

For the world can be a lonely place. Is there an answer for loneliness? For making friends, and keeping them?

Yes. It consists in tackling the problem *simply*. Some people will go to great effort to impress others, to make friends for themselves. But they are not wise.

You cannot make, and keep, friends by assuming a false face. If you put on a false face—a *poker face*—it causes people to wonder what is behind it.

The surest way to make friends is to show what is in your heart. Stop covering up the real, inner you with a poker face. Instead, remember the four women who, refusing to wear a poker face, have enjoyed friendship.

FRUSTRATION

Q. How do you overcome frustration?

A. First we must define the word. Every one experiences one kind of frustration or another every day, but it is there to stimulate us to rise above it, to solve a problem, not to yield to it. When crushed under it, we feel the kind of frustration you are talking about, a chronic type of negative feelings.

We are creative artists when we let our servo-mechanism solve ideas and problems. But too many of us jam our creative mechanism with worry, anxiety, fear, trying to force a solution with our forebrain, the seat of our thinking, but not the seat of execution. This jamming of our creative servo-mechanism doesn't serve us at all. It inhibits us from our goal, putting a roadblock of negation in front of us, creating frustration.

There are five roadblocks of frustration.

1. *We worry not only before making a decision but after.* We carry this extra fifty pounds of worry on our backs all day.

The cure? We express anxiety before we make a decision—not after. There are, let us say, five ways to answer a problem. At this point anxiety is creative as we choose which road to take. Once we do choose, however, we stop worrying and call upon the confidence of past successes to guide us in the present. However, when we call upon failures of the past to guide us in the present, we create immediate frustration.

2. *We not only worry and fret about today, we worry about yesterday and tomorrow.* This sets up the pattern of instant frustration because we

183

call upon past failures and future apprehensions to guide us in the present. But we can't think positively with negative feelings any more than we can think negatively with positive feelings. The cure? Think only of today. Every day is a complete lifetime. Forget yesterday: lose it in the vacuum of time. Tomorrow doesn't exist; when it comes it is another today. Let your servo-mechanism do what it can do well: respond to the present. You try try try—now now now.

3. *We fail with frustration because we try to do too many things at one time.* This creates tension instead of tone, spasm instead of comfort. When we try to do too many things at one time, we try to do the impossible.

The cure? Don't fight relaxation. Join it. Learn to do one thing at a time. This brings relaxation. This frees you from the burden of hurry and failure.

4. *We wrestle with our problems twenty-four hours a day without letup.* We carry our problem from our office to our home to our bed. It creates tension that produces frustration.

The cure? Sleep on your problem if you are unable to solve it. Sleep *on* it, not *with* it. Let your success mechanism work for you when you hit the pillow as you recall past successes.

5. *We refuse to relax.* We don't know what it is. We just know the word, that's all. The spasm of repeated worry produces the spasm of frustration. You can't have someone relax for you. You've got to do it on your own.

The cure? You sit in a room of your mind, and you relax there to cut the electric circuit of distress.

Relaxation overcomes frustration. Don't think it. Fight for it. Do it—NOW!

FUNCTIONING

Q. What are the steps I should take to function at my best?

A. 1. Since we are goal-striving beings, we function best when striving for some useful goal.

2. And we express happiness in the successful achievement of this goal.

3. Happiness can be, and should be, a goal in itself, like breakfast in the morning, and we should strive for it as aggressively as we would for food.

4. Deliberately, as a creative mind watcher, seeing the difference between the happiness habit and the unhappiness syndrome is more than a palliative. It has practical value because we should always remember we are built for success and it is our right to choose what is best for us, and the happiness habit *is* the best for us—a mental habit we can cultivate without imposing on others. In other words, we reach for happiness, remembering not to step on the toes of others, not stepping on our own toes with negative feelings.

5. We must also remember the obvious. We cannot be happy and successful all the time. Problems beset us every day. Why make them worse with increased fears, feelings of inferiority, resentment, uncertainty, that prevent us from achieving our goal?

6. Unhappiness destroys self-respect. We have no right to let it push us around. We owe it to our own stature of dignity.

7. We must understand that happiness is not something we earn or deserve. There is no morality involved in it any more than in breathing,

any more than in survival. And it is not a reward for being unselfish.

8. The act of unhappiness is selfish in that it destroys our worth.

9. The act of happiness in a special moral sense is unselfish in that in making us what we can be, we automatically become more understanding and therefore less selfish toward our fellow man.

10. We must think of unhappiness as painful and evil because it makes us less than what we really are.

11. Happiness, on the other hand, makes us rise to what we really can be.

Remember the words of Robert Louis Stevenson:

"To be what we are, and to become what we are capable of becoming is the only end of life."

GOD

Q. Is God dead?

A. My belief is this: When people say God is dead they are not aware of the fact that they are saying that they are dead and that something within them is dead.

Human nature is such that in too many instances when we are at fault it is so easy for us to blame someone else and, if we get tired blaming someone else, we may blame God.

With all the battlefields all over the world—Vietnam, the Middle East—the area where three great religions came into being—we are apt to blame others, even God, forgetting that the greatest battlefield since the beginning of man has been within himself: the battle with his negative feelings.

Resentment, the twitch of the tensions, the gout of the mind, the daily cancer within us that robs us of our security and dignity, the termites of nothingness that bore holes within us, leaving us empty as human beings. We must tear down this wall of Jericho, down, down, down so that we can see the image of ourselves in God's Image.

What do I mean? I mean this. The business of living is to rise above a blunder, rise above negative feelings, reach our full stature of self-respect, and then share it with others.

Success or happiness is contagious. You can share it with others, pass it on to others, for when you reach fulfillment you express the God-like quality within you. And it cannot remain hidden within you. You have the responsibility to share it with others. You belong to yourself, to your family, and also to community, country and world.

Is God dead? He is alive in the hearts of all of us and we have a moral and spiritual obligation to share our knowledge with others.

There is no police force great enough to police the world—within the framework of the U.N. or without it. You must first police yourself —the negative feelings within yourself. You must control them and rise above them.

Wouldn't it be wonderful if one day the U.N. would have a world forum on: Is God Dead?

HAPPINESS

Q. Can you make a habit of happiness?
A. Yes. The ingredients that make up the state of happiness are:

1. Smile. Smiling can become as natural as breathing air. Learn to smile at least once or twice during the day—more if it is a great day.

2. Be cheerful. Think of some past success. Use the confidence of that past success in your present undertaking.

3. Be part of humanity. Be friendly toward other people. The world longs for friendship.

4. Stop criticizing yourself—and stop criticizing other people.

5. Don't let your opinion color facts in a negative way. I mean don't let some unhappy past smother the present. Forget yesterday. You live today, refusing to permit the negative feelings of yesterday to prevent you from reaching your goal in the present.

6. Learn to react as calmly and intelligently as possible to the day, no matter what happens.

7. If you fail today, remember that tomorrow is an extension of today. Try again the next day. Happiness is the capacity to rise above failure.

8. Know your capacities. When you limit yourself to what you can do, then success is yours. Don't try to be someone else.

Q. What do you mean when you say you can spread happiness?
A. We have all heard of communicable diseases. But have you heard of communicable happiness?

Yes, communicable happiness exists, too. And there are Typhoid Marys of Happiness, people who spread communicable health—the opposite of the Typhoid Marys who spread illness.

There are certain signs by which you can recognize the Typhoid Marys of Happiness. These signs are:
1. Sense of direction.
2. Sincerity and understanding.
3. Compassion.
4. Courage.
5. Self-respect.

6. Confidence.
7. Self-acceptance.
8. Cheerfulness.
9. Optimism.
10. Faith in self and in God.
11. Desire, will, and never-failing positive ability to help others.

These are the Typhoid Marys of Happiness. They spread health, and by spreading it, they are even more infected by health and happiness themselves.

We all can have these qualifications. We can make them our own, one by one, and become Typhoid Marys of Happiness. We become mind watchers, dig beneath our mistakes and find treasures underneath—our assets that give us the means to achieve happiness and spread this happiness to others.

How important it is today to discover the secrets of outer space. How much more important it is, perhaps, to be the mind watchers discovering the inner space of our minds, ferreting out the guilt and hurt feelings that distort our self-image and make us less than what we are, rising above failure to discover that we are successful not from the successes we achieve but from the failures we surmount. It brings happiness, a happiness we are anxious to share with others.

This should teach us one of the great lessons in living—that we can be enriched and ennobled by our scars rather than destroyed by them. We then become Typhoid Marys of Happiness. We then become part of a great adventure in staying young. Remember the words of Horace: "Seize now and here the hour that is, nor trust some later day."

And if we become Typhoid Marys of Happiness and then infect only ten others—and they in turn infect ten more—think how rapidly communicable health and happiness can spread all over the world!

Remember that happiness is the only product in the world that multiplies by division.

Q. What is your definition of happiness?
A. Happiness is a state of mind or habit where we have pleasant thoughts a greater share of the time. It is a built-in mechanism within us. To understand this better, it might be well to realize that we also have a built-in worry mechanism. These are not two separate entities like two ears on the head but they are interlocking processes that work daily in our lives, and when we begin to understand who we are, we alone can decide which mechanism we want to use for our purposes because we can control them. We can make a habit of worrying, or of being happy.

Worry, like happiness, is also a state of mind, in which we throw on the screen of our minds the failures we had in the past and thereby build pictures of failure for some new goal we are undertaking. We have a forebrain, which makes us different from the animal. This forebrain situated behind our forehead is the center of our desires, our goals, our hopes, our sense of achievement, our sense of fulfillment. And when we have a goal in view, we call upon the tape recorder of our midbrain that has registered our past experiences—good and bad—and depending on what we choose from this tape recorder we will go forward toward this goal either with a happy, winning feeling or with a negative feeling that we will fail even before we start.

Q. How can there be abundant living in these fretful, frenetic times?

A. Recently an author friend of mine told me this story:

One morning he found himself depressed. He felt scooped out, depleted. There was an edge of mockery in his mood, like two beautiful bookends with no books between them.

He walked about the grounds of his farm, filling his lungs with pure air. He paused before a grape arbor, surveying the heavy clusters of purple Concord hanging from the vines. The fantastic abundance in Nature. Year in and year out, with no assistance from man, drawing only from the eternal life forces of the good earth, the sun and the rain, and placing its bounty upon the vine for man.

He paused before an apple tree. He saw tier on tier, heavy limbs laden with fruit, though a tree he had never even pruned. Luscious ripe apples for him, for his friends, for his neighbors, for the birds that woke him at dawn, for the little animals of the field.

He surveyed the sheer miracle of abundance.

Other vistas, other greens, more fruit, more abundance.

Who can tally the generous yield, the never-ending abundance—grape, apple, pear, peach, plum on the vine, on the branch, on the ground, spilling over, enough to fill any void. Even the one inside man.

In the world of abundance how can anyone be hollow?

He walked back to his desk, no longer feeling depleted.

My point is that there is abundance within ourselves to make us happy if we remember:

1. We came into this world to succeed, not to fail.

2. We have a self-image within us, filled with

abundance, if we use the confidence of our past successes in the present to reach our goals.

3. Every day is a life in itself filled with abundance if we have a proper image and if we have a useful goal, no matter how small, every day.

4. We rise above failures and mistakes of yesterday, opening the door for abundance in living in the present.

5. We remember what Euripides said: "Enough is abundance to the wise." And this means that abundance never leaves when we share our abundant happiness with others.

HUMILITY

Q. What is humility?

A. Recently I was in a jet on my way from New York to London. We flew from the stars in the night to the rising sun of a new day, and I overheard a man and his wife talking in front of me.

She said: "What a beautiful sight! How insignificant it makes me feel!"

He said: "You mean how grateful we are to be alive in this universe."

This made me realize the meaning of humility. For the purpose of humility is not to make us feel passively insignificant, but actively important.

Great men like Einstein and Gandhi were humble not because they were self-disparaging; they were self-confident about their knowledge and their contribution to humanity.

Humility is not self-denial. It is self-affirmation. It is a blending of success and failure in which we keep our failures in proper perspective in the past, and successes in proper perspective in the present. We let neither dominate us. It is the balance between not trying to be more than we are or less than what we are, not trying to be superior or inferior. It is poise in that we don't inhibit ourselves by past failures, nor do we brag about our present successes. It is our emotional thermostat. It keeps us alive with self-respect.

I once was with an editor friend of mine and he noticed that I was unhappy. A story of mine had been turned down by a magazine. He said: "Maxwell, what gave you the idea that you could be successful as a writer overnight. You'll get many rejection slips before you succeed."

The editor taught me humility. I did succeed in time by overcoming errors instead of letting errors overcome me.

Humility has these eight ingredients:

1. Sincerity. We are sincere with ourselves and with others.

2. Understanding. We understand our needs and the needs of others.

3. Knowledge. We know who we are and we don't have to keep up with the Joneses.

4. Capacity to listen. We thus learn from others.

5. Integrity. We know we are born to succeed, not to fail.

6. Contentment. We are content, not discontented. We are relaxed, not in a state of spasm.

7. Yearning. We have a yearning to improve ourselves.

8. Maturity. We gain maturity with these qualities.

There is no humiliation in humility. It takes time to acquire humility but it brings happiness.

Or, as James S. Barrie said: "Life is a long lesson in humility."

IDENTITY

Q. How do you keep your identity in these times of over-conformity?

A. First let us think about conformity and over-conformity. We all must conform to certain rules. A degree of conformity to regulations is healthy; it keeps life orderly.

We must conform to time schedules—of railroads, airlines, and so on. We must conform to various routines in our jobs and to obligations as citizens.

These conformities are part of civilized living. They are essential for people living in groups. We must have some conformity.

But do we need an over-conformity which imprisons people outside of prison?

You must pay grocery bills, rent, taxes. This is necessary conformity.

But it is over-conformity if you blindly agree to your friends' opinions when you would like to challenge them.

It is over-conformity if you base your life on other people's standards.

It is over-conformity if you "keep up with the Joneses"; "keep up" with yourself.

You keep your identity when you combat these over-conformities. You remain yourself—not someone else.

Maintain your identity as a unique human being; God created you this way.

Q. You say to be yourself or to be "the real you." Yet how can one do this unless he knows what his limitations and capabilities are, i.e., what his real self is?

A. To know the real you when you look in the mirror you must ask yourself, "Who am I? What am I doing to myself, to others? Am I trying to be myself or am I trying to imitate someone else? Or am I trying to please someone else?"

You limit yourself from your true capabilities when you try to be someone else. You then play second fiddle to someone else, carrying this person's image, not your own. When you do that, you fail as a human being. You also fail when you try merely to please someone else and not yourself, because you are trying to live up to someone else's image, not your own.

You slough off the false you when you stop trying to be someone else or to live for someone else. Your real self starts when you become a friend to yourself first before you can become a friend to someone else. You try to become a success with yourself before you can be a success with someone else. You learn to have the love of yourself before you can attain the love of someone else. By love I don't mean narcissism. I mean self-respect.

Self-respect is the beginning of your real self because it implies confidence and courage within yourself, understanding of your needs, and then, the needs of others. It implies a sense of direction to achieve your goals within your limitations and capabilities.

When you know through training what you can do and what you can't do, when you know your capabilities and you limit yourself to these capabilities and do not resort to idle dreaming of being someone else, then you have limitless opportunities to transform your capabilities in achieving realistic goals. One goal after another means limitless possibilities for self-fulfillment.

LONELINESS

Q. I have a terrible feeling of being alone. Why? What can I do to overcome this?

A. We deal with uncertainty all our lives. This creates the feeling of loneliness in all of us—the great scourge of mankind. But the business of living is to bend uncertainty to our will. How? By exercising our rights to live as long as we can— to live and be happy. This means that we are goal strivers and when we reach one goal we start for another. This reinforces you against loneliness as long as you live.

There are three kinds of loneliness: loneliness in relation to the outside world; loneliness in relation to another person; and finally, loneliness in relation to yourself—by far the worst kind of loneliness. It means an image you're ashamed of, an image you can't live with.

Negative feelings produce an unhappy self-image which causes you to move away from the world, from others, from yourself, creating limitation in communication with yourself and the outside world where you belong.

Loneliness means eviction. You cast yourself away from yourself, and this often brings about a kind of stubbornness in refusing to return to yourself.

Loneliness can come from grief when you refuse to let go of it. If this happens, it is no longer a catastrophe of yesterday, but the agony of a lifetime.

You must return to the present. You must refuse to separate yourself from yourself, from others, from reality.

The business of living is to be part of humanity at all times, come what may, to return to yourself, rising above failure and grief, communicating with yourself at all times, rebuilding a new self-image you can live with, an image you can be proud of because you can see it grow as tall as you want it to be. You see it grow NOW, TODAY as you search for goals you can achieve, remembering that no one can make you lonely without your consent.

MOODINESS

Q. How does one deal with moodiness?

A. We all act differently on different days. We may even react differently on different days to the same things. One day, when operating, I may act pleasantly to nurses and assistants. Another day I may be grouchy and severe.

We all have these ups and downs which we call moods—emotional cycles—which depend on the image we have of ourselves as we meet the pressures and challenges of living.

At low periods we become more critical at times—critical of others and of ourselves. We are more irritable and care little about other people. We are depressed, unhappy, ashamed of our self-image. We have temporarily lost our self-confidence, our understanding, our self-respect. Low periods are thus periods of unbelief.

The high periods are periods of hope and excitement, periods of belief and self-confidence; we exultantly tackle the day's problems to reach our daily goal with assurance. Here we have a self-image we are proud of; one we can live with.

We feel on top of the world until we dispose of the surplus energy we have stored, then, subsequently, we may fall into another slump of depression and discouragement. Up and down. You should understand that your behavior depends on your self-image, and that this image can change back and forth like your face, depending on whether it is tense or relaxed.

Since your moods are part of the natural business of living, no matter how dismal the outlook may seem to you when you are low, remember this: You will feel better presently if you can reactivate the success mechanism within you.

At this stage of depression, use your imagination. Sit down in a chair and relax. Go into a room of your mind. See in your mind your past successes. Picture them and feel them. This will help you improve your self-image, returning to you confidence and happiness.

NEGATIVE FEELINGS

Q. How do you overcome negative feelings?
A. The answer, I believe, is in the following letter which I received from a hockey player:

> I have played quite a few years of ice hockey . . . in both Canada and the United States. I have never had a disappointing season except for the winter of 1966–1967. It seemed that everything I did worked against me. I could not score goals or make passes. I even couldn't concentrate on playing a good game. I went through fifty games of agony; pressing harder and harder to play well and score goals but to no avail. My season's output was a lousy six goals in 50 games. I was on the verge of quitting the game even though I knew that my conditioning was good and my body strong. My position on the team was uncertain. I had not produced, but I wanted to play

for the United States World Hockey Team in the World Games held in Vienna, Austria.

A business associate of mine, in a casual conversation, mentioned the book *Psycho-Cybernetics* and how it improved his thinking. He recommended it to me and I bought it with the idea that it might help my hockey career as well as business.

I immediately began applying the techniques to improve myself. I sat down in my lounge chair each day in my office and turned the lights off. I reenacted as many situations in as many games as I could remember, especially in the games when I failed miserably. I discovered that in almost every game that I recalled I distinctly remembered experiencing great emotional fear of being injured while playing. As a matter of fact this fear seemed to dominate every situation that I could recall. The answer to my difficulties seemed so simple to me as I sat in that dark room. Why, I was constantly thinking of being injured and this preoccupation of my mind was enough to throw my entire game into failure after failure.

I immediately began to replace this negative feeling and thought with a positive feeling and thought. I recalled every situation in the past when I had done well and had scored goals. I relived the excitement and the great feelings of being a winner, when I scored those goals. I replaced these thoughts, eliminating the fear of injury.

I honestly repeated this system each and every day through February and March of 1967. Things did not change immediately but I knew in my own mind that they would . . . and change they did! I moved from my bench position as a reserve to the starting line up. I began scoring goals and playing the game with new enthusiasm. It seemed as though I had never played the game before. My success was unbelievable.

My name appeared in headlines. I kept scoring the winning goals when two months back I could not do the job. An amazing turnabout. I continued to lead the team in scoring with eight big goals during the European tournaments . . . most of them key goals which won the games. 1968 is the Olympic Year and I know exactly what I am going to do to be on that team!

PRESSURE

Q. How do you live with pressure?
A. First, you must accept your periods of weakness. This is of basic importance in dealing with pressure because you cannot always feel strong.

Unfortunately, many people—especially men —feel they must always be strong.

If you cannot accept weakness, you may crumble in crises. For, if you must always be strong, you overburden yourself and are liable to feel weak.

Under pressure, anyone will at times feel uncertain and take no action when he should act.

Under pressure, anyone may become arrogant and impossible.

You must accept these forms of weakness under pressure. You must try to overcome them and steer yourself into positive channels, but first, you must accept them. If you don't, you have no floor under you to cushion your falls.

So, first accept your weaknesses—because this will move you toward genuine strength. Accept your negatives, then use your assets to reactivate your success mechanism.

Q. How do you know you are yourself with all the pressures and tensions facing you?

A. The business of being your true self consists in standing up to the pressures—the tensions and problems—of the day. Problems will always confront us. They are there to surmount. That is what enhances our integrity as human beings, giving muscle to our spiritual and intellectual fibers. Success doesn't mean being "successful." Success means the capacity to rise above a problem, a failure, a tension, a corrosion, a conflict.

How do you know yourself? You begin to know yourself when you give yourself the chance to develop and make your image grow when you tackle problems. If you let negative feelings overcome you and complain that life was unkind, that you were born unlucky, then you are not yourself. Then you become less than what you really are and you make your image shrink in size.

How do you know yourself? You look in the mirror and ask yourself this question. And you, not someone else, must answer it. You answer it by knowing you are a combination of frustration and confidence, happiness and despair, and you resolve to mean something to no one but to yourself and through this resolve you have the desire to amount to your true self. This desire gives you the direction to reach your goal of finding the better part of you, the true you, refusing to be less than what you think you are through some error of the past.

You are yourself when you are true to yourself. Then life has meaning.

PSYCHOANALYSIS

Q. Can psycho-cybernetics be a substitute for psychoanalysis or are they two separate techniques that are unrelated? If they are related, how are they related?

A. Psycho-cybernetics is no substitute for psychoanalysis. It is quite different from psychoanalysis, which delves into the past, whereas psycho-cybernetics delves into the present. It may be of value to delve into the past, but you are a different human being today and what you do with your life today is more important regardless of the negative feelings and mistakes of yesterday. You learn to rise above them today.

I suppose both can work jointly, but psycho-cybernetics can work without the other because psycho-cybernetics is self-analysis without using another party. You and you alone take stock of yourself—of your assets and of your liabilities—and you make the decision NOW that you are going to do something creative with your life.

Psycho-cybernetics considers the average psychoneurosis the result of just a bad habit and the whole principle of self-image psychology that I advocate is that you have a self-image and that you can change your self-image for the better. You and you alone can change from a bad habit of frustration into a useful habit of confidence.

Here is a letter written to me by a distinguished psychiatrist:

> It was a great source of pleasure as well as professionally gratifying to read your remarkable book on psycho-cybernetics which caught and held my interest to the end and which promises reward on a pragmatic level far beyond the average. I am aware of how psychiatrists for the most part are chary of contributions to their field from regions of science outside their immediate echelon of knowledge, but the lively style and lucid articulation of ideas in your book must certainly disarm the a priori resistance of the most

hardened psychiatric recluse, and arrest his thinking on the subject in a trice.

As one whose principle engagement in psychiatry down thru the years has been that of psychotherapy of the neuroses, I became many years ago—following a defection from the straight Freudian line—drawn by those schools of thought which pushed the importance of the self concept as crucial in therapeutic advance—Horney, Fromm, Robbins, *et al*—but in spite of assiduously studying the theoretical formulations and even doing control work with various of the scholiast disciples I was never satisfied with the application of theory to practice as it shaped up, and was always malcontent with the varying 'technical' modalities for solving the problem which I tried to organize myself on a purely independent basis.

The fascinating utilization of Norbert Weiner's theories which you have so auspiciously put to work appeals to me as a solution on the therapeutic working level which promises great things. The clear and straightforward presentation of the dynamics as outlined by yourself is easy to grasp, and in addition any intelligent patient should be able to utilize the book either as a therapeutic instrument per se, or in conjunction with any self-oriented system of psychotherapy. I shall look forward to having many copies of the book close to hand for service in the aforesaid area.

Once again allow me to thank you for a rewarding and stimulating professional experience.

PSYCHO-CYBERNETICS

Q. What do you mean by the word: *Psycho-Cybernetics*?

A. Cybernetics is derived from a Greek word

kybernetes, meaning a helmsman, a man who steers his ship to port. The word I coined, psycho-cybernetics, means steering your mind to a productive, useful goal. People with negative feelings are likely to steer themselves off course. But psycho-cybernetics is a creative process aiming at self-fulfillment.

Salvadore Dali, the famous Spanish artist, once gave me a painting of his concept of psycho-cybernetics. In the center is a world divided into two parts. Half the world is in shadow from frustration, and here man's image has shrunk to the size of a small potato, with man walking away from life and from himself into the dark corners of his troubled mind, while below a ship without sails flounders in the stormy seas of frustration, never reaching port. The other half of the world is in sunshine from confidence gained from past successes, confidence used in man's present goal to reach fulfillment. Here man's image is ten feet tall, and walks toward the sun, while below a ship sails through calm waters, about to reach port.

What is this port? Peace of mind. Each of us is composed of many people—particularly of two opposing forces of frustration and confidence —and psycho-cybernetics means using the success instinct within us to reach our full stature of self-respect. One step beyond worthwhile positive thinking, is positive *doing*. You take a constructive thought and turn it into a creative performance, moving toward your goal, refusing to let negative feelings throw you off course.

RELAXATION

Q. How does one relax in these uncertain times?
A. We have many games which are vehicles for

physical relaxation, but what I am considering now is the mental and spiritual relaxation which brings with it physical relaxation.

Every generation speaks about uncertain times. Born in uncertainty, living in uncertainty, we pass on in uncertainty. The business of living creatively is to bend uncertainty to our wills as we reach our goals and a sense of fulfillment. We live successfully by rising above our tensions; we can do this effectively if we practice the art of relaxation.

There are five cardinal points to relaxation. Each one is difficult to do but you can do it; and the rewards are tremendous.

1. Forgive others, with no sense of condemnation. A clean, clean slate—no forgiveness on the installment plan. I love you today but can't stand the sight of you tomorrow—that is not forgiveness. A difficult task, but worth fighting for.

2. Forgive yourself for your errors or blunders. Another difficult task, but you can do it. Forget the blunders of yesterday and make it habit to live fully *today*. To err may be a human failing, but to forgive is a human achievement. Shakespeare said: "To forgive is divine." Still, who is asking you to be divine? Be human and achieve your fulfillment as a human being.

3. Keep up with *yourself*, not with someone else. Trying to imitate others merely forces you to play second fiddle; anyway, you can't be someone else without tension. Every day you must try to make your own self-image grow; this you can do.

4. See yourself at your best; stop concentrating on your worst. You are at your worst when you torture yourself with feelings of frustration every day. You are at your best when you practice confidence every day, using the confidence of your

past successes in your daily undertaking. You have a choice; exercise it.

By frustration I don't mean the frustrated feelings all of us experience during the day. By frustration I mean chronic frustration, when we carry fifty pounds of extra weight on our mental back every day because we failed in some undertaking deep in the past, making a habit of negation, continually feeling insignificant in the present. You must forget yesterday and you forget by substitution, thinking and working toward your present goal. The more you think of reaching your present goal, the less time you will have for the worries and heartaches of yesterday.

5. Give yourself an assignment when you sit in a quiet room and use your imagination. See in your mind a geyser letting off steam, a symbol for you to let go your tensions of the day, to break your electric circuit of distress—even for a moment—so that you can then renew your energies for the demanding tasks that lie ahead of you when you face the new today.

RELIGION

Q. Where does religion fit into psycho-cybernetics?

A. One person at a religious college asked me if psycho-cybernetics takes the place of religion. No, not at all. The principle of psycho-cybernetics involves the ways and means of steering your mind to a productive useful goal—to fulfill yourself. Every basic tenet of every religion teaches self-fulfillment. You should be better than what you think you are and you do this not by thinking about it but by utilizing the success instinct within you, the servo-mechanism within you to steer your mind to a creative productive goal.

Psycho-cybernetics is no substitute for religion but it has a spiritual basis behind it. You set goals within your training, within your capabilities, to reach your full stature of dignity and self-respect. Psycho-cybernetics means, in other words, a search for your integrity as a human being—and that is what religion teaches. So all that psycho-cybernetics can do is help you fulfill yourself regardless of your religious beliefs. It makes you a better spiritual human being and therefore makes you more successful in what your beliefs may be.

Young people are looking for spiritual guidance and when they know they can fulfill themselves through psycho-cybernetics they will fulfill themselves as human beings—whole persons keeping themselves whole, physically, mentally, psychologically, and spiritually, all the equipment that will make them return to their place of worship. Why? Because they have a stake in themselves, to amount to something. When they have dignity, they have compassion. When they have compassion, they have humility. When they have humility, they have the courage to be themselves, to stop building walls of resentment. They must learn to tear this wall of resentment down, to tear this wall of Jericho down, so that they can see their image in true focus, an image in God's image.

Is God dead? As far as I'm concerned, NO! There is no answer for people in existentialism— that we live a life of futility. This is inconsistent with psycho-cybernetics for the simple reason that if you succeed, if you fulfill yourself as a human being, you then express the God-like quality within you. God is within you if you want to see yourself and believe in yourself. I believe you came into this world to succeed.

SELF-IMAGE

Q. What do you consider man's most important asset?
A. His self-image. Each of us has a mental picture, a blueprint of himself. This blueprint determines how you act in your relationships with other people. To find life reasonably satisfying you must have an image you can live with. Before you can find yourself acceptable to others, *you* must find yourself acceptable. You must believe in yourself.

When your self-image is confident, you express yourself and function at your best. But when this self-image brings you shame and fear of failure, you stifle creative expression and walk away from reality and others *and yourself* into a dark tunnel in your troubled mind. Hurt feelings and resentment follow. You then find it difficult to get along with others—and with yourself.

Our self-image is our key. If, remembering the confidence of past successes, we use it in our present goal, chances are good we will succeed. If, however, we fear making a mistake, remembering our past failures, we fail before we even start.

Q. Can people really change?
A. They can—if they can change their self-image. This is their greatest asset. We all can use a change for the better. And, since most of us are in the habit of short-changing ourselves because of our guilt feelings over some blunder of the past, we must remember that we are usually better than what we think we are, and that we came into this world to succeed, not to fail.

We must have the desire to change. We must remember that one thing common to all mankind is the desire to live, not just exist—live and be happy. This is a goal common to all. If we remember this when we feel inadequate, and if we refuse to lose sight of this great goal, we then will refuse to let negative feelings sidetrack us from it.

We must systematically remember that this self-image doesn't rule us; we rule it. We systematically recall a time in the past when we were successful and happy and we systematically imagine we are that person *now* by concentrating on our past confidence in the present.

Every day is a day for improving your self-image. This is your first daily goal of fulfillment when you get up in the morning and look at yourself in the mirror. You ask yourself who you want to be that day? You must answer. If you saw yourself as unhappy, see yourself happy, remembering that no one can make you unhappy without your consent. Imagine yourself confident within your capabilities; make the confidence you once had the confidence that belongs to you now. Use it. Fight for it.

Q. How do I start to change? What is the first step?
A. The first step is to realize that you *can* change for the better. How? You look in the mirror and take stock of yourself. You say: "Who am I? Because I failed in some undertaking, am I therefore a failure? Or am I a person born to succeed when I use the confidence of some past success in my present undertaking? Who is the real me? Am I afraid of making a mistake, afraid to be anything but perfect, forgetting that there is no human being alive who is always perfect, for-

getting that I'm neither superior nor inferior? Who am I? Am I a mistake maker? Yes. And I'm a mistake breaker. Success is not just being successful but the capacity to rise above a blunder."

Who are you? A person of frustration or a person of confidence? Both? Yes. Within the mirror of your heart are reflected the many people who you really are, but in essence you are a combination of frustration and confidence.

As you look in the mirror, you are seeing a motion picture of yourself, a living, breathing X-ray of who you are and what you can do. You remember that you came into this world to succeed and not to fail, that success and happiness belong to you like your heart or your eyes. You grasp for it without stepping on other people's toes, without stepping on your own toes with negative feelings.

So you see yourself in the mirror. How do you start to change? You come to grips with yourself. No evasion, no double-talk, no games of make-believe. You have a moral and spiritual commitment when you see yourself in the mirror to answer the question of who you are.

You are both frustration and confidence, but you can't be both at the same time. You have to decide which way you want to jump. You should jump on the side of confidence. You make a habit of it, day in and day out. You live in the present —your present goal. The more you concentrate on achieving your present goal through confidence, the less time you will have for worrying about the failures of yesterday.

Q. Is there a danger of too much attention to the self-image lapsing into conceit? Where do you draw the line? What is the difference between a healthy use of psycho-cybernetics and conceit?

A. In the first place there is never any danger of paying too much attention to one's self-image—because it is an attempt to understand who you are and what you are doing. When you are doing something you do it creatively without stepping on someone else's toes, without stepping on your own toes with negative feelings. The trouble is that not enough attention is paid to one's self-image. There would be less heartache and less conceit in the world if more attention were paid to oneself when looking in the mirror—to see the face behind the face, the face of your mind, and learn to do something creative for yourself. Being aware that you can rise above a mistake means confidence. This is quite different from conceit, which is lack of confidence expressing a false sense of superiority to cover up some form of inadequacy.

When you look at yourself realistically and learn more about yourself in a creative way by avoiding the pitfalls of negative feelings, you do something creative. When you look in the mirror and see only your face and nothing else and you adore your face, expressing a narcissistic complex which is self-defeating, you are involved in a display of conceit that has no foundation in reality, leading to nothing. Confidence means self-respect that you share with yourself and try to thrust upon others. Confidence is creative; conceit is destructive. Thus a healthy use of psycho-cybernetics to find your true worth and rise above problems and defeat and develop confidence makes you aware that conceit hurts the one who uses it.

Q. If I have a proper and healthy self-image, do I have any limitations of capacity?
A. If you have a self-image, that is, if you see

yourself as you and not someone else—neither superior nor inferior, a person who is a combination of successes and failures—if you accept your weaknesses and forget them today, since these weaknesses were from the past—if you concentrate on your assets, using your confidence every day, setting goals for yourself realistic in terms of training and capabilities, living in the *now*—then you have a proper, realistic self-image that will guide you to your goal. Then you have a self-image you can live with, and you can forge ahead toward your goal utilizing your servo-mechanism to achieve fulfillment.

You limit yourself only in what you can do creatively within your training and capacities. This means that your limitations are, in a sense, limitless since you are using the best that is in you to achieve success. Having limitations doesn't mean you are limited in your capacities. If you stick to what you do rather than fret about what other people want you to do, then your goals are limitless. One goal after another, not two goals at one time. When you reach one goal you start on another. This enlarges your capacities to the full.

Q. What is the relationship between one's self-image and one's conscience?
A. The development of a satisfactory self-image implies the constant battle we wage within ourselves against the negative feelings that rob us of peace of mind.

The battleground is not only in the world around us—Vietnam, the Middle East—but in the world within us. We wage an endless internal war against our failure mechanism. The battleground is there behind us when we look in the mirror—

even if we are not aware of it. We must make ourselves *aware* of this eternal warfare between our assets and our liabilities. We must prevent negative feelings from steering us off course, away from our goals, with clear thinking and creative mental imagery, with utilization of our success mechanism, refusing to compromise with fear, frustration, resentment.

The strength of our self-image is the strength of our conscience. They are one and the same. Use a few minutes every day to get acquainted with your conscience when you look in the mirror. Learn to know better that face behind your face, that stranger within who can become your best friend. Shakespeare said in *Hamlet:* "Conscience doth make cowards of us all," but I believe it is the other way around. We make cowards of our conscience when we permit hurt feelings to undermine our self-respect.

Now is the time for self-fulfillment. Now is the time to know and feed our conscience creatively as you look in the mirror. No double talk, no evasion, no deception, no make-believe. You are a Michelangelo now, a sculptor of the mind, and now you are chipping off your negative feelings that you put there yourself. The result will be a resurgence toward successful living. You don't think about it; you work on it.

Victor Hugo said: "There is one thing greater than all the armies in the world put together and that is an idea whose time has come." Your time has come. Make your image grow tall, make your conscience clean and bright, the fantastic mirror within you that will reflect the joy within you to others. Not the sorrows, but the joys.

Your image *is* your conscience. Make it clean and bright—*now.*

Q. Have you been part of any experiment with LSD as a way to improve the self-image? Please comment upon your feelings about such experimentation.

A. I have had no part in any experimentation with LSD to improve the self-image. Under proper medical guidance some value may come from the use of LSD, but as far as I am concerned it is of no value in improving your self-image.

Your self-image implies a personal relationship between you and the person within you. It is a face-to-face confrontation before the mirror when you wake up in the morning before you go out into the world. And you don't sit on the fence not knowing what to do about yourself. You have to give the answer: Whether you want to be a success or a failure, whether you want to rise above a mistake or whether you want to complain that the world has been unkind to you. It is an intimate affair, an intimate romance with no interruption from without—whether it be another person or a drug. There is no mystery about the you in you, the person within you, the opinion you have of yourself—your self-image.

If your opinion about yourself has been wrong because of some blunder in the past, you and you alone must rectify it. You don't need a drug to put you in a state of hypnosis to find out who you are; you don't need a hypnotist to find out who you are. You will know who you are if you will know that you can rise above a mistake of yesterday and that you try to live successfully now—and if you fail you start all over again. You learn you have a success mechanism. You overcome failure by using the success instincts within you to succeed. You do it, no one else, and when you

do you have hypnotized yourself into a useful creative habit.

Q. How do you overcome the snobbishness of too
great a self-image?
A. In the first place a proper self-image is inconsistent with snobbery. A self-reliant image, that
you can live with and be proud of, has the ingredient of humility, not of snobbery. Snobbery implies
an unsatisfactory self-image—an image with a
scar on it.

What makes some people snobbish? In the
first place they want to feel important; to them it
means progress from an inferior position, an attempt to get somewhere. But this thinking is er-
roneous. To attain a superior position with sense
is one thing; to do so without sense is another.
Thus if some do not attain recognition by proper
means they resort to the futile tactics of snobbery,
by forcing their supposed superiority on others,
thinking that their pretentious pose is legitimate.

Snobbery consists of (1) conceit, (2) emptiness, (3) pettiness. Snobbery can be a form of
conceit derived from a false sense of superiority
thrust upon people by virtue of birth, education or
wealth when these assets are not utilized properly
and to full human advantage because they haven't
done anything for the individual. As Shakespeare
said: "Conceit in weakest bodies, strongest works."
Thus snobbery can be a form of inferiority which
makes the afflicted pick on people, serving notice
on them that they want to be noticed.

The snob thinks he derives a certain amount
of security when he indulges in this prank, but it
is a delusion. Superior people are humble and
thankful for their accomplishments and never

force their egos on others. Their egos don't need recognition; they have that already.

Snobbery is thus a form of self-inflicted emptiness which disfigures the self-images of people and makes them small potatoes. The best one can claim for snobbery is that it is a form of pettiness that scratches for attention but leaves no impression—like a finger scratching marble. When people resort to snobbery they foolishly, without dignity, tell everybody: "Look folks, I love *me!*" And this is failure, the failure mechanism within people, making them less than what they really are.

The best way to cope with snobbery is to remember that, when snobbery tries to seduce you, you should become a snob to it. You should stick your nose up in the air, ignore it as if it were dust. It will make you feel that you have accomplished something worthwhile; improving your self-image. Then you have a right to indulge in a little bit of self-admiration because you have lived up to your self-respect.

Q. I have an associate who, I am sure, has the capacity to do much better in his work than he is doing. What can I do to help this man reach his potential?

A. The value of creative psycho-cybernetics and self-image psychology is that not only do you improve your self-image but when you do you pass on your knowledge to others. This is the beginning of friendship; first you are a friend to yourself, then you give part of your courage, your confidence, your understanding, your self-respect to others. It is, in a way, another form of group therapy in which the personal rewards for doing something for someone else are beyond computation. We are islands within ourselves but we also belong on the mainland to our people, our community, our country, our world. We have a moral commitment to others, and we must respond to this commitment.

How do you respond? By getting into conversation with this associate, telling him what a rewarding experience psycho-cybernetics has been to you. Have him read the book. Discuss segments of it pro and con just as you would discuss a football or a baseball game—there are winners and losers, and losers in sports forget about yesterday and try to win *today*. Let him know that he is more than a mistake—a mistake-maker but also a mistake-breaker. That's what creative living is all about. It becomes a great adventure for both of you.

Do this, too, with your wife or with a child. Perhaps the art of constructive conversation has been sadly neglected at your home—with each other, with friends. Start the ball rolling *now* and you will suddenly find that you are more than you thought you were, that you are *somebody*, a *creator*, a plastic surgeon removing inner scars from people.

Q. Doesn't one's self-image hinge upon at least a hint (and probably more) of conceit? This is normally recognized as a character flaw. What do you think? In building self-confidence is there a danger of overconfidence?
A. Conceit is a character flaw and if people who resort to it would realize that it expresses some form of inferiority they would learn to rise above it. All of us can. It is absolutely false that one's self-image hinges upon conceit. Learning to believe in yourself when you rise above a blunder in no way means that you become conceited. It means that you have found the better side of yourself. What do you really find when you improve your

self-image—conceit or self-respect? You find your self-respect and when you do that you never become conceited simply because self-respect means confidence and when you have true confidence you share it with others. This means you have humility, and humility is the reverse of conceit. When you are conceited you put a scar on your self-image. You remove that scar with confidence which implies humility.

Conceit is a character flaw; confidence is a character asset. Develop your confidence and forget the fear of overconfidence.

With all your confidence you can never be perfect. You are bound to fail in some undertaking now and then and this will prevent you from being overconfident. It will also stir you to rebuild your confidence for the new tasks and the new goals ahead.

Q. Why is there such a tendency for people to continue throughout life with the same self-image without making appreciable change, even though that image is quite inadequate?

A. Too many people don't realize that they can change their self-image. If you believe you're a failure, you'll prove to the world you're a failure. You perform according to what you believe your self-image is. Understanding your self-image is the difference between success and failure.

One reason it has been difficult for people to change their personalities and habits is that they have directed their efforts at change to the circumstances rather than to the image itself. But you can't think positively about a situation if you have a negative concept about yourself. The core of changing the personality lies in changing the self-image.

Let me tell you this story:

Helen, seven, overheard her parents say, on hearing her play the piano, that she was clumsy with her hands and would never become a good pianist. She accepted this as the truth and whenever she played the piano she played clumsily to confirm the truth of what her parents had said. When she was fifteen she played awkwardly. Moreover, when she used her fingers in cooking and sewing she used them clumsily, too.

I said to her: "My dear child, you can't be held responsible for the actions of someone else even if they are your parents. Maybe that particular time when they heard you you weren't your best. That doesn't mean that you can't improve."

She got the message. Two years later she played the piano well. Not only that, she cooked better and her fingers were agile when she sewed.

Changing her opinion about herself, she changed failure into success. She refused to call herself a failure simply because she didn't do too well when her parents heard her play that day when she was seven.

A change in personality starts when people realize that they are better than they think they are and that they can improve their self-image every day of their lives.

Q. How does one quickly achieve peace of mind?
A. You start with your own self-image. No escape each day into the room of your mind will refresh you if you do not approve of yourself.

Tranquility of the spirit means a stronger self-image. Here are three ways to guide you toward peace of mind.

1. Realize that peace of mind is a possibility; make it a basic goal.

2. Escape each day—if only a little. Seek out enjoyable activities, and stop holding grudges.

3. Work to build your self-image.

To be wealthy in spirit, you must strengthen your self-image. You must see yourself at your best —in your imagination.

You must recapture your past successes—in your imagination.

To have peace of mind, you must build strong beliefs. You must believe in yourself, believe you are a person of dignity.

This self-belief is essential to peace of mind. Keep working to develop this positive attitude toward yourself. Then, when you wake up in the morning, you will enjoy your day. Because you are at peace with yourself.

Because, day after day, you are creating the best world you can inside yourself.

Q. From two college students:

1. I'm flunking out of school and I don't think I'll succeed afterwards. Help!

2. What do you feel is the most confronting internal friction that a college student has?

A. In a recent survey one researcher reported that over 90 per cent of college students, male and female, don't like themselves. They haven't a proper self-image and in an effort to find themselves, find a career for themselves, reach the threshold of adult life with a goal in view, they are beset with genuine problems. Not being able to achieve fulfillment immediately, they don't like themselves.

Most young people live exaggerated lives; they are in a hurry (I can say that for myself when I was young). Perhaps that is an asset rather than a liability, a challenge to develop the mental muscles of students to rise above problems; anyway, they most assuredly do for by far the greatest percent-

age don't flunk out but come through with flying
colors.

Recently at the invitation of the Dean of the
College of Business Administration of the Louisi-
ana State University, I gave a talk to 1,275 students on how to create a desire for learning. My
talk was on psycho-cybernetics with emphasis on
improving the self-image and learning how to
stand up under stress.

Here is a letter from the Dean about the
lecture:

Dear Dr. Maltz:

May I express to you my sincere appreciation of the outstanding lecture which you pre-
sented to the 1,275 students in our Introduction
to Business course on Wednesday, January 11,
1967. The University is indebted to you for the
excellent contribution which you made to the
educational experience of these students.

The attention and applause which you received from the students in the live class session
were unmistakable evidence of the interest and
value which your lecture had for these students.
However, I want you to know that the reports
from the other six classrooms in which your lecture was received by closed circuit television were
unanimous in their praise. In fact, one instructor
in one of the TV classrooms reported that the
students became so engrossed in your story about
your trip from the seventeenth floor of your apartment building to Kennedy International Airport
to catch a plane to California during the New
York Electrical Blackout that they applauded
you when you reported that you reached the
airport just in time to catch your plane. I am
confident that your message will prove personally
valuable to many of the individual students in
this class. The student who heard your lecture

should certainly now have a better understanding of the importance of discovering for himself his own strengths and limitations and learning how to control his own movement toward his own specific goals. This proposition certainly has direct relevance to the learning process and to motivation for the individual student in college.

It was a pleasure and a privilege to have the opportunity to get to know you and you will receive an invitation to lecture to this class again next year.

Best wishes to you.

This points out the following:

Does a student go to college to learn or does he go away from home to be away from home merely to make social contacts? Does he go to learn superficially merely to pass, get a college degree in order to get a job?

This, to me, is the most confronting internal friction a college student has.

He (or she) must look in the mirror, confront himself honestly, learn something about his self-image by asking himself who he is and what he is doing. No double talk. He, and he alone, must answer the questions and when he realizes that success consists in trying to be successful and that it is within him to succeed and go about it in a hurry he will stand up to the tensions within him.

In all probability when a student in Denver, Colorado, said: "I'm flunking out of school and I don't think I'll succeed afterwards. Help!" he didn't realize, as he must now, that he can change his self-image. He must help himself, refusing to let negative feelings destroy him in life even before he has started life. He must realize that there are no bad students in life. They can make themselves worthwhile. He must remember that he came into this world to succeed and not to fail. He must remember that he has within him the desire to live and be happy and do something about it—in a hurry.

Clark Kerr, formerly president of the University of California, has this to say:

"Exaggeration is one that fits the new generation. It has exaggerated itself. It has been exaggerated by the news media. It has been exaggerated and also used, for their own purposes, by the left and the right. And as a result seldom in history have so many people feared so much for so little reason from so few."

So what? If they are exaggerated in their lives they can do something constructive about it NOW. The great majority will do well when they realize that they and they alone make the decision about themselves, that they can't be a friend and a success with others until they are a friend and a success with themselves. I speak to students. I'm on the visiting faculty of Purdue University. I talk in other universities all over the country. I have faith in students because hidden by the exaggeration without is the faith and respect they have for themselves within. The majority will do well.

SEX

Q. Have we false conceptions about sex?
A. Often, yes. As a plastic surgeon, I have operated on many celebrities, including heralded "sex symbols." I also know other well-known personalities: statesmen, executives, people in the arts fields.

Now sex is a somewhat private area, so one can only guess at answers. Still, I see little if any correlation between real sexual fulfillment and the ballyhoo of sexual imagery.

Thus the individual selected for commercial sex showcasing may or may not have emotional qualities that lead to real sexual fulfillment.

The sexually fulfilled person, I woud say, feels an inner contentment and knows how to give and take—without narcissism.

Such a person feels concern for other people in a fundamental way. This person may not have the kind of physical image one sees on magazine covers or paperback jackets—"sex symbols" of today.

For sex is more than what meets the eye. It is a wonderful feeling which the person with the healthy self-image can feel, added to physical sensations for someone of the opposite sex.

SIN

Q. What is your interpretation of sin?

A. I'm not a man of the cloth and I don't know what sin is. This is not an evasion but a belief as a medical man. When you bring a child into the world and you spank his backside and he opens his mouth for the first time and lets you know he has arrived—when as a medical man you see the wonder of birth—you can't help but believe that there is a new human being without failure. You can't force upon him without his consent that he came into this world to fail and that there is nothing he can do about it. I have traveled all over the world lecturing on psycho-cybernetics to young people, to people of all ages and of all faiths, and it is difficult for young people in particular to believe even before they reach the threshold of adult life that they have already erred. They won't buy it. Why should they?

Youth demands that they should have a

chance and a chance they will have whether adults like it or not.

People must learn to forgive themselves, forgive others, see themselves at their best not at their worst, and keep up with themselves, not with someone else.

As a doctor helping people get rid of their outer scars, and what's more important their inner scars, I don't know what sin is but I do know what failure and success are. I know that people are capable of making mistakes but, thank God, they are capable of rising above their mistakes.

To me one of the great cardinal sins—if we are to use this word—is not making a mistake but the refusal to rise above a mistake. The other real *sin*, as I see it, is to refuse to forgive others.

SLEEP

Q. I will be graduating this May from college, B.S. in nursing. In July I plan to go for my master's.

For the past two or three years I have been having sleep problems. I am unable to go to sleep until two, three or four A.M. I don't have to be upset. Just can't relax or turn off my brain. But it is a desperate feeling and I will be unable to do well in school if I don't get help. I worry about school much too much anyway.

A. The first principle for sleep is to establish a routine, a cycle, and live by that cycle. This means you have to get to bed at the same hour every night. That's the least you can do for yourself and it is by far one of the most effective methods, far better than mechanical gadgets that constantly repeat a monotonous sound or imitate the sound of the surf or other sleep provokers such as counting sheep that keep many people awake, or spraying pleasant odors in your bedroom. The best of these artificial methods is a lukewarm bath before bedtime.

The best advice is to learn the art of relaxation. Control your worry, and rise above it. It takes courage to brush aside for the moment the mental or economic burdens of the day so that you can sleep and be fresh to tackle them the next day.

And to relax your mind and spirit at night when you turn out the light and go to bed should not be as difficult as we make it. You spend one third of your life, eight hours every day, sleeping and, by the very nature of it, by the very repetition and habit of it, you should become proficient in the art. Make it a business to sleep better just as you make it a business to do a better job every day when you meet people. Do a good job too when you meet yourself in bed at night. Remember you deserve it, you are entitled to it, regardless of your problem. Sure, people who are sick may need pills during their illness, but those who are well should avoid pills as much as they can. To get in the habit of taking a pill is just as bad as not being able to go to sleep unless you count sheep.

Sleep is a good habit, a natural habit to preserve the body economy. Keep it as a good habit for your own well-being. You have about eight hours a day after work before you retire. Use a few moments of that precious time and think rationally of the things you ought to do to get a good night's sleep; prepare your mind by having the proper relaxed attitude toward sleep so that when you hit the pillow you will fall asleep.

It is best not to read any book before retiring; it encourages you to stay up longer and read more, or think about the book when you turn out the lights. And try not to take that sleeping pill—try hard.

I recently left San Francisco at 10:30 P.M. to get to New York early the next morning. A friend of mine—a business executive—was on the plane.

"Doc, got any sleeping pills?"

"I have a few in my bag."

"Give me one."

He swallowed the pill with a little water, then said: "How about you, Doc?"

"I never take any. I keep them for patients."

Early next morning my friend shook me and woke me up.

"We're in New York, Max. Damn it, I was up all night trying to get to sleep. I just couldn't with that awful snore of yours."

SMALL POTATO

Q. I always feel like a small potato. How do I overcome this?

A. Carlyle said: "Society is founded on hero worship." We see it in our lives. We cheer the winner in a prize fight, the actress for a fine performance, the politician who wins an election. Our hearts are set on success. Yet man is a paradox and performs various daily acts inconsistent with achieving importance. He persists in doing the very things that will make him a small potato—*unimportant*.

Once a patient, a woman of forty, traveled across the country from California to see me. I looked at her but could see nothing but worry on her face.

"What's the trouble?" I asked.

"My scar," she said.

"Where?"

"On my lip." On her lower lip she exposed a tiny scar.

This woman had looked at this tiny scar so

227

often and brooded about it so much that to her it was a hideous defect.

Most of us receive little wounds from people in our daily struggles and we exaggerate their significance when we brood over them. They become so great to us, though unimportant, that they make *us* unimportant.

We are so concerned with being small potatoes that I thought it would be of value to jot down what to do to become a small potato.

How do you become a small potato? Coddle your regrets. Long for the past. Complain every time things go wrong. Be petty about your neighbor's good fortune. Stay hurt about small matters. Stay disappointed twenty-four hours a day. Under all circumstances insist on being absurd.

Don't stop brooding over your grievances for in a year or so everyone will forget them. Don't devote your time to worthwhile actions and feelings. Don't dare to think any positive thought or of any wonderful affection. Don't remember that every scrap of time is worth saving.

Follow these precepts carefully and I can assure you that you will become the smallest of the small potatoes.

But life is too short for you to be a small potato. The cure is obvious. Turn your back on the failures of yesterday and today.

Live creatively today—with a goal for each day.

Then you will not be a small potato.

SUCCESS

Q. How do you explain to loved ones who have given your life direction your need to make your own success your way?

A. You respect their wisdom in guiding you properly, but there comes a time when you must respect your own wisdom. You can't have strings attached to you forever. They must not demand it of you nor dare you demand it of yourself.

Every human being has his own image. He must take the calculated risks in living to enlarge and enhance his image; he must learn to guide himself without interference even if he makes a mistake. He must learn to rise above his own mistakes on his own terms.

Their way is not your way and your way is not their way. Their blunders are not your blunders and your blunders are not theirs. True friendship means the respect for one another's self-image, without interference.

The world of people—friend and stranger alike—is made up of a world of distinct self-images.

Think of it as a U.N. of distinct self-images with your right to move into the world on your own volition without interference, with a right to creative adventure on your own with full knowledge of the risks involved and of the rewards when you reach your goal your way.

You are your own Columbus charting the world before you for your self and, when you succeed, you enjoy the success with others.

Have a round table discussion with your loved ones. No pretense, no double-talk; just honest expression of each other's right to exist on each other's terms.

If they love you, they'll understand and agree.

If they mean only that they want to shield you from the suffering they experienced, tell them you have to take your chances in life your way.

If they resent this, they don't love you. They love themselves. If you don't stand firm for your rights, you don't love yourself and you'll never find your real image.

Q. How does one become more efficient?
A. Personal efficiency implies movement forward with intensity, courage, and confidence—with energy and with an inquiring mind to separate fact from fantasy. It is a wholehearted enterprise to reach a goal within your capabilities, also an enterprise against negative feelings. It implies a yearning to be better than what you think you are, knowing what to do and what not to do.

Personal efficiency starts with a personal confrontation in the morning when you wake up and look in the mirror to see who you are. You respond creatively to this confrontation, getting off the fence the first few minutes of the day and saying to yourself:

I shall remember to concentrate on my goal for the day.

I shall remember to do one thing at a time.

I shall remember to live in the NOW with discipline.

I shall remember the Who, What, Why, When, How, and Where about my goal.

I shall remember to persist in my goal; I will refuse to let doubt and fear sidetrack me.

I shall remember that there are three eight-hour periods in the day: eight hours for work, eight hours for rest and relaxation, and eight hours for sleep. I resolve to live creatively in work, play, love, and worship.

I shall remember that frustration is the thief of time.

I shall remember that before I can learn to manage others, be a friend to others and have the respect of others, I must learn to manage myself, be a friend to myself, and have respect for myself.

I shall remember to make the most of every minute by reactivating the success mechanism within me.

I shall remember this blueprint of the better me at all times.

Q. What creates the inner drive that keeps you on a consistent track of success?
A. The first thing you remember is that you are a human being—*somebody*, capable of error, but also capable of rising above it.

You remember that failing in one undertaking does not make you a failure. No one is perfect; no one is successful 100 per cent of the time.

You remember that no one tells you what to do but yourself and that you have one desire common to all human beings: the desire to live, not merely to exist, to live and to be happy. No one can stifle this desire but you yourself. You must refuse to permit anyone to crush this desire that is the life blood coursing through you. You are an actor in life endowed with a creative force, with a subconscious servo-mechanism which will guide you to success. You are not merely a reactor, reacting to negative feelings, prostrate before them. Negative feelings mean no goals.

You remember that you are a goal striver and striving means that you try—and you will get there if you try. And, if you fail, you try again.

You refuse to let blunders sidetrack you for, when you do, you put a deformity, a scar, on the greatest treasure you will ever have—your self-respect.

Your self-respect is the incentive within you that keeps you moving toward your goal, moving somewhere, on the road to success—even if you fail now and then. You are the goal. YOU are the success—before you even get there, moving toward self-fulfillment.

Q. My belief is that your book *Psycho-cybernetics* has kept me from going into a period known as a slump. I've been able to eliminate negative thoughts by using the principles of your book. Yet I am confused by you saying that it is normal to have these slumps. I disagree. You have eliminated them for me and changed my whole outlook on life.

A. I am happy indeed you feel that way, but life is such in these frenetic times that we are all burdened now and then with negative feelings. We can't be successful all the time. All people, no matter how successful, have their periods of depression, their ups and downs. It is a natural process even if we learn to live creatively. Being aware of this in no way prevents you from changing for the better. As a matter of fact it gives you added courage to stand up under stress when it occurs.

Still, none of us can be perfect all the time. When we succeed in an undertaking, we are perfect then and only then. That does not mean that we are insured or guaranteed perfection the next day, because when you achieve one goal you don't rest on your laurels but you start for another goal. Life means one goal after another. And if we don't reach all of them, we needn't despair. The best batter in baseball never hits home runs all the time.

If I have helped you eliminate slumps for good, fine, but remember: Don't be disappointed if now and then you are overcome with one. Being aware of it and knowing that it is temporary and that you can rise above it is the beginning of creative living, the beginning of success, the beginning of changing your outlook on life for the better.

Q. How would you describe man's servo-mechanism?

A. Each of us has a success mechanism within us that works subconsciously to help us reach our goal of success and happiness. As an example, if I want to pick up a pen on a table, I do it without effort. But once, at the age of one or two, when I wanted to pick up the pen, I zigzagged to it with many unnecessary motions. I didn't know the easy way to do it. Then, watching others, I learned how and have done it successfully ever since. I forgot the wrong way of doing it, remembering only the successful way. This success pattern is registered in the tiny electronic computer in your midbrain, a tape recorder that holds all your past experiences, good and bad.

When I want to pick up the pen, the desire to pick it up, the goal, starts in the forebrain behind the forehead. This is the seat of our desires and hopes, our sense of fulfillment and achievement—our goal center. Calling upon that tiny electronic computer in my midbrain, I tap the successful way of doing it, forgetting the wrong way. I don't know all the muscles involved in picking up the pen; I do it subconsciously by calling upon the servo-mechanism within me, the success mechanism. To repeat, this performance is done *subconsciously*, not by will power, not by our forebrain—the center of our goals, not the performance of the goal.

In the same way we can pick up success, remembering that when we reach for success we must not step on others.

Q. Who in your opinion is the most successful man in the Twentieth Century? Is this man the man who has made the most significant contribution to the common good of mankind? If not, who is this man?

A. My answer may surprise you. *You* are the most successful man in this century—if you fulfill yourself.

The criterion for success is different with different people but certain basic requirements are common to all forms of real success in living.

First of all, by success I don't mean prestige symbols. If you carry someone else's image, you're out of luck immediately because you're playing second fiddle to someone else. Success starts when you accept yourself for what you are, knowing you are neither superior nor inferior.

Making a living is vital; we must succeed financially for ourselves and our family but that is only one aspect of success. The other aspects are:

1. S: Sense of direction for goals.
2. U: Understanding.
3. C: Courage.
4. C: Compassion.
5. E: Esteem.
6. S: Self-confidence.
7. S: Self-acceptance.

You don't measure success in terms of money alone. You remember the seven other aspects.

Perhaps you don't have to remember all the letters that spell out success if you will remember the word CONFIDENCE. When you remember your confidence of past successes and use it in your present undertaking to reach your goal, it becomes second nature with you. Then all other aspects of SUCCESS will follow.

Will your success mechanism direct your thinking and doing to a point of self-respect that may border on conceit? No. Confidence implies humility; you stretch out your helpful hand to people less fortunate, which can never mean conceit.

Success, like happiness, reaches its finest moment when you share with others. What you make, you might lose; but what you give, you will always have.

What is the measure of complete success? I don't believe anyone reaches complete success all the time. When you reach one goal, you start for another. And when you fail, you start all over again.

Success means trying, trying, trying, doing, doing, doing, NOW NOW NOW.

Every human being has a distinct self-image; to make this self-image grow tall every day is more than a personal adventure. It is the greatest adventure of all time—especially when you help others too.

Thus, when you fulfill yourself, you become the most successful man of the Twentieth Century.

TOMORROW

Q. How do I overcome procrastination?
A. Though we are born equal, we inherit different characteristics; still, one thing we inherit in good measure is the ability to put off things until "tomorrow." Many of us hold onto this "talent" for a lifetime.

We have no courses in schools or colleges on doing things tomorrow. Yet, if one should give such a course, few of us would not take it. No sleeping in this class. This doubtless would be the most popular course on the campus.

Now, I do believe in the art of leisure, but this is different from leaving things until "tomorrow." Indeed, idle people have the least leisure for it is the reward of work that prepares the body and mind for tomorrow.

To do things tomorrow is a negative philosophy because no one has ever seen "tomorrow."

Nevertheless there is a special form of philosophy which teaches How To Do Things Tomorrow constructively.

Group together certain qualities that you feel are detestable. For example, you don't like hate. Add a few others to the list—such as insolence, bigotry, envy, malice, indolence, boredom, revenge, slander and finally, lack of faith in yourself, in others and in God.

As soon as you become poisoned with any of these emotions, now is the time to get lazy and say it can wait—till tomorrow. This is a positive tomorrow habit.

I have answered this question indirectly, I guess. But one way you overcome procrastination is by becoming aware of the ludicrous evasion it involves. In making you aware of the evasiveness of the common tomorrow philosophy, I hope I am helping you to overcome procrastination.

TRUTH

Q. How do you appraise yourself?
A. It is remarkable that we are least objective in appraising ourselves. Masterly in our understanding of others, we may still be irrational in understanding ourselves.

From what I have read, even the great Sigmund Freud, whose creative and courageous work has had such impact on our thinking, could not completely fathom the mysteries of *his own mind*.

And so it goes with others.

The physicist, master of technical concepts, may have a distorted, untruthful view of *himself*.

The judge, who dedicates his life to justice and truth, may know little truth about *himself*.

Now, what is your truth about yourself? Do you feel inferior because you never made as much money as someone else? Is your truth that, as a single woman, you are a total failure because you didn't marry?

Or do you believe a physical feature shows your inferiority? A long nose? A "weak" chin?

Or do you destroy yourself with other "truths"?

Too many people see only negation when they think they see "truths" about themselves. They block off joy because they are so critical of themselves; their "truths" are distortions.

Stop short-changing yourself, and de-hypnotize yourself from your ridiculous attacks on yourself. Try to be objective; give yourself some justice for a change.

Then you may be able to move forward into a more creative life.

UNHAPPINESS

Q. How do you break the unhappiness habit?
A. Put up a mental mirror in front of yourself in the room of your mind. The image you see there is yourself as others see you, as the world sees you.

Study the image carefully; be a creative mind watcher. Look at it without sympathy or favor but quite objectively—for that is how the world looks at you.

Now, are there any minutes of the day when you have reason to be humiliated by the image's behavior? Or, to coin a word, let us say *unproud* of its behavior?

Yes, alas, there are these minutes, too.

And most of these minutes you are ashamed of are the ones you are devoting to a foolish, childish, time-wasting or health-destroying habit.

You are looking at yourself now as the world sees you. And of course you wish the world to see you at your best. You do not wish to look foolish, childish, or weak-willed.

There is only one way to avoid that: end the habit. You are a mistake maker, but, thank God, you're also a mistake breaker. That is the essence of creative mind watching.

Look into that mental mirror when the habit next gets its grip on you. And, of course, I mean that common habit of ours—the unhappiness habit. The mirror makes an ugly sight then.

How much better—and how easy—to make it a sight that will please the eyes instead! We substitute the happiness habit as we visualize the ingredients of the happiness mechanism.

And mark my word! You will find that the habit of unhappiness almost magically has gone.

To help you break the unhappiness habit, remember the words of James Russell Lowell: "The misfortunes hardest to bear are those which never come."

Q. Can you make a habit of unhappiness?
A. Yes. By refusing to let go of the mistakes and the frustrations of yesterday. No one is perfect. You are neither superior nor inferior. Capable of blunder, you are also capable of rising above it. Unhappiness becomes a habit through constant

worry, constant fear, constant negative feelings we invoke from the past in an undertaking in the present.

These are the ingredients that express the state of unhappiness. Remember them only to avoid them.

1. A frown on the face instead of a smile.

2. Sad instead of cheerful.

3. Not friendly to others.

4. Critical of others, critical of ourselves. Intolerant, lacking understanding.

5. Not successful in understanding the personality we don't want to be.

6. Letting our own opinion color facts in a negative way.

7. Not learning to react calmly to things every day.

8. Living on negative feelings of the past and the present.

Remember that no one can make you unhappy without your consent.

WEAKNESS

Q. Why do men punish themselves so much?
A. They do when they think they have committed the "crime" of weakness.

Many American men punish themselves, because their self-expectations stem from fantasy more than from reality.

Many men expect themselves to live up to absurd ideals of strength. He may also expect himself to be totally fearless—even in situations where fear is normal. He will wear a stoical mask to hide fear from others. He scorns tears.

This is a deprivation because crying—in

times of bereavement—is natural. The "strong" man who never cries makes himself weaker—not stronger.

Such a man is always in hiding—more than an escaped convict fleeing police—concealing his human weaknesses. When will he show fear or indecision? Or perhaps he will make a mistake? Then he will reject himself and project another unrealistic image of himself into his mind until once again something pierces his armor. He can never win.

If you expect yourself to be such a "tough guy," you must resolve to change.

You must feel you are worthwhile even if your muscles do not bulge, even if you sometimes are afraid.

Just as you cherish your strengths, you must accept your weaknesses.

You can change; you must. This is what psypcho-cybernetics means, steering your mind to a productive, useful goal.

WEEKEND

Q. What steps should you take to "psych" yourself up Monday morning after a nice weekend?

A. In the first place a weekend or any vacation, for that matter, should not only be a period of relaxation where you escape momentarily from the tensions of the day so that you can renew your energies for the tasks ahead of you, but simultaneously a rest period, a period of escape, which you use not to run away from yourself but to get to know yourself a little better. As Thoreau said, a retreat can be of value to increase the soul's estate.

Weekends or vacations shouldn't mean running away from yourself but rather returning to yourself by learning to be yourself and not trying to be someone else. You use your rest period to understand your rights, to reactivate the success mechanism within you, and to select realistic goals that you can reach if you will refuse to let negative feelings or the failures of the past sidetrack you.

In other words, a weekend of fun is fine but it should also remind you that every day you can have a weekend of profit—a vacation, a retreat—when home from work during your eight hours of relaxation you sit in a quiet room of your mind for a few minutes and take stock of yourself. This will in no way interfere with your pleasure; it will, rather, enhance it.

Making a habit of this is easy and when you do you don't have to "psych" yourself up Monday morning after a nice weekend. For you've been "psyching" yourself up every day, knowingly.

When achieving a goal of this kind that belongs to you, you can say to yourself that you have had no "lost weekend" but a "found" one.

WINNING

Q. How do you become a winner?
A. I'd like to tell you about the Kentucky Derby.

Shortly before 4:30 P.M. on the first Saturday in May at Churchill Downs the world's fleetest three-year-old thoroughbreds paraded onto the track for the 93rd "Run For The Roses." Over 100,000 spectators stood and sang in the rain as the band played: "My Old Kentucky Home."

Excitement mounted as the horses reached the starting gate, and people tensed as the starter shouted: "They're off!" For the Kentucky Derby is a most exciting sporting event. For the many thousands who watch the Derby on TV or hear it on radio, it is in a class by itself.

Over 100,000 people yelled their lungs out at Churchill Downs. The contest, a gruelling test, was over quickly—in two minutes—and to the jockey who won the "Run For The Roses" it was a marvelous prize.

Two minutes and it is over, and one man becomes the champion.

Can you be a winner, a champion in your own Kentucky Derby? I believe you can; I believe all of us can.

Our "Kentucky Derby" is a special kind that we can win every day of our lives. How? Every day we allot two minutes to ourselves. We sit in a quiet room and become a racing contender. We see ourselves running for our self-respect. We imagine we run toward our goal—without holding ourselves back with negative feelings. Every day is a new day, a new lifetime for us when we become winners and use the confidence of past successes in our present undertaking. When we do this, when we keep our eye on our self-respect, we never lose, we are always the winner in our run for self-fulfillment—the greatest "Run For The Roses" of mankind.

And do you know something? When you run your own Kentucky Derby it is always sunny—for you can find the sun within yourself if you will only look.

Q. Is there a quick capsule formula for winning?
A. There are few absolute rules in life.

Still, we must live by rules; so here are two rules for developing a winning spirit.

1. *Get tough*. Get out into the world and try to survive the hard knocks of living. Get in touch

with other people; relate to them. Stay in the world without giving up your freedom.

Winning seldom comes immediately. Everyone knows defeat sometimes. You must be tough.

2. *Set goals*. How can you win if you don't know what you want? You must set goals.

This will give you a sense of direction. If your goals mean something to you, you will feel enthusiasm for attaining them—and this is a winning feeling.

Your goals need not be concrete. Some important goals may be invisible; thinking through an idea, forgiving a friend, imagining past successes.

If you set meaningful goals, you are on the way to a winning spirit. If you are tough enough to attain them, then you are there.

WORRY

Q. What do you mean when you say: Worry should be a challenge?

A. We all worry. But worry should be a challenge to stand up to our full stature of dignity. Stress is part of living and we must learn to cope with it, not let it destroy us. We never solve anything by carrying worry from our business to our home then to our bed. No one forces you to do it. We must learn that when we do this we burden ourselves with the *extra* unnecessary tensions that pile up on our back and weigh us down, making us less than what we are, making us walk away from ourselves, making us become the small potatoes we actually aren't.

There are other extra unnecessary stresses that create extra unnecessary tensions—resentment, hatred, bigotry. These feelings hurt most the one who feels them.

Our happiness mechanism is within us ready to work for us if we learn to communicate with ourselves first, if we become a friend to ourselves first before we become a friend to other people.

Unhappiness prevents this glorious adventure in human fulfillment. It is up to us to make it a practice for five minutes every day to have pleasant ideas and memories, those fine feelings of usefulness and kindness that make us part of humanity.

We must make a habit of this as we would of breathing exercises every day. Habits are responses which we have learned to perform automatically—like tying your shoelaces or brushing your teeth. And it is just as easy to have the happiness habit as the unhappiness habit. The choice is yours.

YESTERDAY

Q. You said that yesterday is unimportant and we should forget it. Shouldn't we learn from our mistakes of the past? Yesterday isn't entirely irrelevant.

A. I didn't say yesterday is irrelevant. We learn from the mistakes of the past. We learn to be on guard not to repeat the same mistake. We also learn something more important from the past. We remember our successes and we use the confidence of past successes in our present undertaking, making a habit of this. It thus becomes second nature with us and we can tap this confidence instantly when we need it (and we need it all the time) creating for us one of our greatest assets, instant confidence.

If, however, we can't forget yesterday's blunders, or the frustrations and worry about them every day in our lives we carry the burden of fifty extra pounds of continual chronic frustration on our mental backs and continually living in the past, fearful of failure in the present, we develop the habit of instant frustration.

Now and then we can return to the past for a moment when we walk into a room of our mind— into a gallery where we see the faces of joy and sorrow on the walls of the past—but there comes a time when we must return to the present.

Keep yesterday in proper perspective. The more you live in the present, reaching realistic goals, one after the other, the less time you will have to relive the errors of yesterday. This is how you forget the negative feelings of yesterday—by substitution.

ABOUT THE AUTHOR

MAXWELL MALTZ, M.D., F.I.C.S., received his baccalaureate in science from Columbia University and his doctorate in medicine from its College of Physicians and Surgeons. One of the world's most widely known and highly regarded plastic surgeons, he has lectured before the University of Amsterdam, the University of Paris, and the University of Rome. He has been Professor of Plastic Surgery at the University of Nicaragua and the University of El Salvador. In addition to his nine other books and eight plays, including *Adventures in Staying Young* and the bestsellers *Dr. Pygmalion* and *Psycho-Cybernetics,* Dr. Maltz has made numerous contributions to professional medical journals all over the world.

Bantam
On Psychology

☐ 28037	**MEN WHO HATE WOMEN & THE WOMEN WHO LOVE THEM** Dr. Susan Forward	$4.95
☐ 34366	**SIGNALS** Allen Pease (A Large Format Book)	$7.95
☐ 26401	**MORE HOPE AND HELP FOR YOUR NERVES** Claire Weekes	$3.95
☐ 27376	**HOPE AND HELP FOR YOUR NERVES** Claire Weekes	$4.50
☐ 26754	**PEACE FROM NERVOUS SUFFERING** Claire Weekes	$4.50
☐ 26005	**HOW TO BREAK YOUR ADDICTION TO A PERSON** Howard M. Halpern, Ph.D.	$4.50
☐ 27084	**PATHFINDERS** Gail Sheehy	$5.50
☐ 27106	**PASSAGES: PREDICTABLE CRISES OF ADULT LIFE** Gail Sheehy	$5.50
☐ 27043	**THE POWER OF YOUR SUBCONSCIOUS MIND** Dr. J. Murphy	$4.50
☐ 34574	**GOODBYE TO GUILT** Gerald Jampolsky, M.D. (A Large Format Book)	$9.95
☐ 34367	**TEACH ONLY LOVE** Gerald Jampolsky, M.D. (A Large Format Book)	$7.95
☐ 27333	**LOVE IS LETTING GO OF FEAR** Gerald Jampolsky, M.D.	$3.95
☐ 25822	**WHAT DO YOU SAY AFTER YOU SAY HELLO?** Eric Berne, M.D.	$4.95
☐ 27158	**PSYCHO-CYBERNETICS AND SELF-FULFILLMENT** Maxwell Maltz, M.D.	$4.95
☐ 27087	**CUTTING LOOSE: An Adult Guide for Coming to Terms With Your Parents** Howard Halpern	$4.50
☐ 26390	**WHEN I SAY NO, I FEEL GUILTY** Manuel Smith	$4.95

Prices and availability subject to change without notice.

Buy them at your local bookstore or use this convenient coupon for ordering:

- -

Bantam Books, Dept. ME, 414 East Golf Road, Des Plaines, IL 60016

Please send me the books I have checked above. I am enclosing $ _____
(please add $2.00 to cover postage and handling). Send check or money order
—no cash or C.O.D.s please.

Mr/Ms _____

Address _____

City _____ State/Zip _____

ME—1/89

Please allow four to six weeks for delivery. This offer expires 7/89.